The First
World Series
and the
Baseball Fanatics
of 1903

·The First World Series

and the Baseball Fanatics of 1903

Roger I. Abrams

NORTHEASTERN UNIVERSITY PRESS • *Boston*

Northeastern University Press

Copyright 2003 by Roger I. Abrams

Library of Congress Cataloging-in-Publication Data
Abrams, Roger I., 1945–
The first World Series and the baseball fanatics of 1903 /
Roger I. Abrams.
p.   cm.
Includes bibliographical references and index.
ISBN 1-55553-561-5 (cloth : alk. paper)
1. World Series (Baseball) (1903).   2. Baseball—Social aspects—
United States—History—20th century. I. Title
GV878.4 .A27 2003
796.357'646–dc21   2002153049

Designed by Gary Gore

Composed in New Baskerville by Book Production Resources,
Tampa, Florida. Printed and bound by Maple Press, York, Pennsylvania.
The paper is Sebago Antique, an acid-free stock.

Manufactured in the United States of America
07 06 05 04 03   5 4 3 2 1

To Fran, as always

Contents

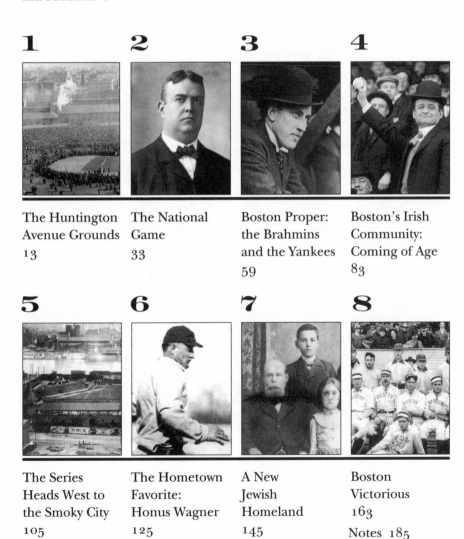

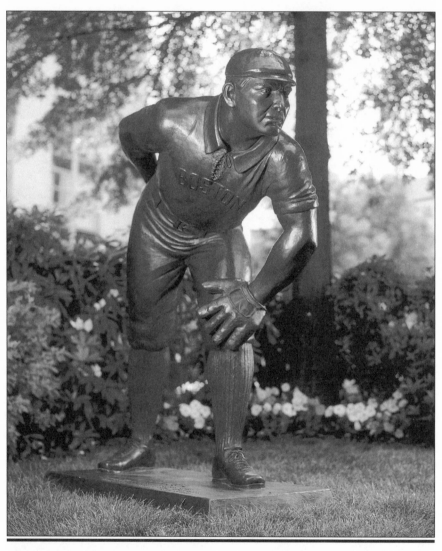

CY YOUNG

This statue of Cy Young was erected near the site of the pitcher's mound in the old Huntington Avenue Grounds on what is now part of Northeastern University's campus.

Preface

At the center of the Northeastern University campus on Huntington Avenue in Boston, down a path named World Series Way, there is an imposing statue of Cy Young. On the mound, with his foot on the rubber, Young peers in for the sign, undoubtedly from his longtime catcher, Lou Criger. One can imagine the Boston Americans positioned behind their great hurler, led by the Hall of Fame third baseman Jimmy Collins, the captain and manager of the Boston nine. At first the statue seems out of place, erected on a knoll in front of Churchill Hall, where Northeastern's president has his office.

A campus information sign explains the significance of the Cy Young statue: In 1903, on land now part of the Northeastern University campus, stood the Huntington Avenue Grounds, the home field of the Boston American League club, later named the Red Sox. In October 1903 those hallowed grounds were the venue for baseball's first World Series, between the pennant winner of the National League, Pittsburgh's Pirates, and their counterpart in the American League, the Boston Americans.

For someone who has enjoyed baseball since childhood and who has written two books about the law and business of baseball, the attraction of this important historical event on the Northeastern campus fifty yards from my office proved irresistible. What was baseball like a century ago? Who attended those postseason contests? What role, if any, did baseball play in a boisterous city filled with new immigrants?

The standard texts on baseball sketch the outlines of the story. Before the 1903 season, the National and American Leagues entered into the Cincinnati Peace Agreement, settling their economic conflict and joining the rival circuits under a single governance system. A postseason tournament between the victors of each league seemed a natural consequence. (Only later did I learn that the agreement had not provided for a World Series — the brainstorm of the owner of the Pittsburgh Pirates.) There are some interesting stories about the loyal fans, including a group of Irish spectators who called themselves the Royal Rooters and were led by an impish, mustachioed saloon keeper named Mike McGreevey.

The local newspapers of the time add a new layer of intriguing facts. There were ten daily newspapers in Boston at the turn of the twentieth century — the *Globe, Herald, Post, Record, American, Advertiser, Traveler, Journal, Transcript,* and *News.* I selected three — the *Globe, Herald,* and *Post* — as a representative sample of the print media of the time. (The other papers carried similar stories of the sporting events.)

According to the contemporary media, the grandstands at the games were filled with representatives of almost all segments of Boston's population at the turn of the century, with the notable exception of persons of color, who were systematically excluded from almost all phases of public life. There were second- and third-generation Irish and some "proper Bostonians" who were listed in the press as among the "notables in attendance." On October 2, 1903, for the second game of the Series, the newspapers reported that Rabbi Charles Fleischer of Temple Adeth Israel attended as the guest of Barney Dreyfuss, the German-Jewish immigrant who owned the Pirates. The press devoted almost as many columns to the shenanigans of some of the spectators, in particular the Rooters, as they did to the happenings on the field. It seemed apparent that there was an interesting story to tell about the events that would draw together so many disparate elements of the Boston community to root in common for nine young men who were playing what had once been a children's game.

Boston in 1903 was a teeming metropolis. The prior decades had seen an influx of immigrants, and the streets were filled with the bustling multitude speaking a variety of languages. It was a time of great technological innovation, although the wealth created by the increased worker productivity was, as usual, not shared equally. Boston's inhabitants looked for entertainment and found in professional sports an exciting and affordable diversion that, combined with hometown pride, converted an audience into "fanatics" who identified with a team that wore the city's name on their shirts.

The story of the 1903 World Series offers a prism through which we might view the social landscape of a century ago. The Series itself was fascinating, filled with greats of the game, such as Pittsburgh's Honus Wagner and Boston's Cy Young, and tragic figures such as Ed Doheny, the Pittsburgh pitcher who suffered a mental breakdown and was committed to an insane asylum as the Series proceeded in Boston.

One preliminary word about spelling. The city of Pittsburgh was sometimes spelled "Pittsburg" before and after the turn of the twentieth century. In 1890, the U.S. Board on Geographic Names decided that for the sake of uniformity all American cities and towns ending in "burgh" must drop the final "h." (Despite the edict, Pittsburgh city ordinances retained the "h.") Citizen protests finally forced the board to reverse its decision in 1911 and restore the "h." For purposes of convenience, I have selected one spelling using the final "h." On the other hand, the word "baseball" was commonly divided into two words before the turn of the century ("base ball"). Sometimes a hyphenated hybrid ("base-ball") was employed. In quotations, I have used the spelling employed in the original document. Otherwise, I refer to the sport as "baseball."

Of course, all books are the product of collaboration. We learn from the insight of others, past and present. I have learned about baseball and about America from too many people to list in any preface. My spouse, Fran Abrams, helped devise this project, researched a significant portion of the social side of this baseball story, and edited the manuscript. Many thanks also go to Joan Murray, Steve Klein, Bill Nowlin, and Deborah Feldman.

**The First
World Series
and the
Baseball Fanatics
of 1903**

Introduction

> The one constant through all the years, Ray, has been base-
> ball. America has rolled by like an army of steamrollers. It's
> been erased like a blackboard, rebuilt, and erased again. But
> baseball has marked the time. This field, this game, is a part of
> our past, Ray. It reminds us of all that once was good, and that
> could be again. Oh, people will come, Ray. People will most
> definitely come.
> —James Earl Jones as Terence Mann in *Field of Dreams*

The 1903 World Series marked the first postseason tournament between the pennant winners of the National and American Leagues of baseball, and it would become one of America's great traditions. After two years of bitter commercial warfare and a peace treaty signed before the 1903 season, the two major circuits of baseball clubs were ready for combat once again, this time on the field and not in the board offices. In 1903, no one appreciated that this postseason event would be repeated annually (with but two exceptions) for a century. Outside of the cities of the two competitors, Boston and Pittsburgh, few took much notice. However, in those cities baseball fanatics were enthralled by the spectacle. The Boston and Pittsburgh newspapers devoted banner headlines and multiple columns of print to the unfolding events on the diamond and among the crowds of spectators. Political, civic, and business leaders joined the throngs of everyday people who would fill Boston's Huntington Avenue Grounds and Pittsburgh's Exposition Park beyond their capacities.

By the turn of the twentieth century, baseball had become firmly fixed as America's national game. It was played by boys and men on urban sand-lots and rural fields. It was a passion that consumed much of the spring, summer, and fall, and occupied the attention of rabid partisans during the long winter months. Baseball was an important part of Americana.

Of course, other events filled the newspapers during the first two weeks of October in 1903. Boston hosted a symbolically important visit from the British Honourable Artillery Company, the artillery brigade that reminded Boston's upper class, the Brahmins, of their Anglo heritage. Jews — both German and the recently arrived Russians, Litvaks, and Galitzianers — observed Yom Kippur, the holiest day of the Jewish year. The Democratic Party of Massachusetts held its nominating convention, once again domin-ated by the sons and grandsons of Irish immigrants. Yet, above all, the "Hub," as Boston is known, was baseball crazy.

The baseball fanatics who followed the daily happenings in the Series, either at the ballpark or in the newspapers, came from many ethnic back-grounds. Like all European Americans, they or their ancestors had immi-grated to these shores. They came as part of ethnic clans and as individuals, as adventurers and refugees. They brought with them the customs and lan-guages of their countries of origin, a variety of work skills, and great cour-age, but generally only modest financial assets. Many scholars have docu-mented their travels and their settlement, but their American experience also included involvement as spectators at the 1903 World Series.

Traditionally, baseball history tells the stories of the men who played the game. Every child who loves baseball knows of Babe Ruth and Lou Gehrig, Ty Cobb and Joe DiMaggio. But the game as a cultural representation is more significant than the men who played it on the field. It fascinates us because we feel that we participate, not by making a shoestring catch, but by rooting for the members of our favorite team, suffering when they lose, glorying in their victories. We, as baseball fanatics, identify with our "hometown" teams, even though few, if any, of the players come from our hometown. (Only one player in the 1903 World Series—the great Pittsburgh shortstop Honus Wagner—played for his "hometown" team.) Baseball "fever," as it once was called, has been rampant for more than a century as generations of fans have passed on their baseball genes.

Although baseball is certainly a profitable commercial enterprise, it is more than a business—it is a socially interactive phenomenon, unlike other forms of nonsports entertainment where the attendees sit passively. Baseball has spectators and rooters, not an audience. At times, baseball fanatics can even affect the outcome of a contest. That may have been the case in the 1903 World Series, when Boston's Royal Rooters traveled to Pittsburgh and resuscitated the failing fortunes of their local heroes.

The 1903 World Series had some superb players—Hall of Famers Cy Young, Honus Wagner, Jimmy Collins, and Fred Clarke, to name just four. It had some unexpected heroes such as Bill Dineen and Deacon Phillippe, two pitchers who reached the apex of their careers that October. Their stories are worth retelling. They also were the sons and grandsons of immigrants who, blessed with extraordinary athletic skill, found work as professional entertainers on the baseball diamond.

Immigrants to America forged a new energetic society with a fascinating social history. Separated by class, race, and religion, they were united by an affiliation to an urban space—to a city. They would form the social and political coalitions needed to govern their city.

Baseball was a cultural event that was involved in all their lives. It was a public activity that attracted a noteworthy, and perhaps unique, diversity of spectators. European immigrants came out to the ballpark to root for the men who represented the cities the immigrants had adopted as their own. Few of the ballplayers and none of the immigrants were natives of that urban space. This game of baseball was foreign to all the new arrivals, yet they quickly adopted America's game as their own.

Waves of Immigrants

The English, Welsh, and Scotch-Irish came to America to populate the British colonies and clung close to the shores of the Atlantic in the seventeenth and eighteenth centuries. They were farmers and merchants, artisans and laborers. They built small settlements that grew into towns and, when swelled by later waves of immigrants, eventually into cities. Their children played games with bats and balls, progenitors of what would later become America's game of baseball. Some moved west in pursuit of economic opportunity and freedom from the confines of urban neighborhoods. They would establish towns in the west, such as Pittsburgh, where factories would produce the materials needed for an expanding American economy.

Millions of European immigrants—the Irish and Germans in the mid-nineteenth century and the Italians, Poles, Russians, and other eastern and southern Europeans at the end of that century and the beginning of the next—came to create a life in a land so different from the one they had left. All immigrants faced formidable barriers. Those who had come to start a new life would have to learn how to survive in an unfamiliar environment. Accommodation required determination. Few had ever lived in crowded urban areas—dirty, noisy, large, and bustling. Others had come for what they expected to be a short stay—to earn enough money in America to make a better life in their home countries. They would have to prove that their work had market value in the growing and changing America. These "birds of passage," typically young men who had left their families behind in the old country, would migrate back and forth across the Atlantic. Only two-thirds of those who came to America settled here permanently.

Europe in the nineteenth century had experienced a dramatic increase in population as infant death rates declined. Governments controlled by the landed and merchant classes offered few opportunities for advancement and social reform, and compulsory military service provided a very good reason to emigrate. At the same time, the world's economy was changing from one dependent on manpower and horsepower to mechanized industry. The instruments of this technological revolution—the telegraph, railroad, and steamship—would also facilitate the mass migration of Europeans to America.

Although conditions in their home countries were harsh, most Europeans had a choice whether to emigrate or stay in the homelands where their families had lived for centuries. European immigrants were not forced to come to America as African slaves were, chained below decks and treated as chattel. Even after making the transatlantic voyage, European immigrants had the option to remain in this country or head back home. While we focus here on the experience of immigrants who chose to come to America, millions more moved within Europe or from Europe to South America and beyond. Immigrants from Asia filled California with inexpensive physical laborers.

For the most part, the Jews of eastern Europe came to America to stay. Only one out of twenty returned to Europe. Although they were not forcibly expelled from the Pale of Russia, the prospect of continuing to live under the threat of vicious pogroms, without the right to buy land or attend school while being subject to induction into the czar's army for an unlimited period of time, made the Jews most likely to establish firm roots in their new American homeland.

For all immigrants, American life required adjustments. There was a new language to learn, a new set of mercantile and social rules to master, and a radically different way of life to absorb. Imagine the amazement of the immigrant who walked out of his sparsely populated hometown village and arrived a few months later in an American metropolis. Everything was alien to these newcomers. They sought to minimize the psychological shock by seeking out friends and family from the old country, searching for the familiar in a land so foreign.

These immigrants adapted to America, and, at the same time, America adapted to its new inhabitants. Those who were the first European immigrants—in Boston, the Yankees and their prosperous cousins, the Brahmins—appreciated the need for more able-bodied workers to help build the nation's economy, while they were understandably wary of the newcomers' strange appearance, customs, and religious preferences. The process of assimilation required mutual accommodation, and it did not go easily.

For the most part, American society has always been segregated by class, race, and ethnic origin. Homogeneous immigrant clusters sat side by side within well-understood boundaries in the neighborhoods of the great cities. Workplaces, including the great manufacturing concerns, also reflected ethnic differences. Immigrants sought out places to live and work where people spoke their language, where grocers sold familiar foods, and where there were opportunities to socialize with those who shared a common language and heritage.

There were times when the boundary lines were crossed. In Massachusetts, for example, young Irish women would work as servants in Brahmin homes. Jewish street peddlers would sell their wares to Yankee housewives. Merchants in city centers would market to anyone with cash in hand. In their nonworking hours, however, the boundaries would reappear. Places of worship remained segregated, as did public amusements and social accommodations such as saloons. Irish Catholics and Boston Brahmins even established their own schools.

The predominant ethos of "boisterous Americanism" prevailed on public occasions. Members of immigrant groups viewed these occasions as opportunities to prove their allegiance to the dominant culture. While they might cheer during the celebration of the Fourth of July, their participation was essentially passive because they could not yet claim "ownership" in the land and its traditions. They were outsiders residing in a country someone else founded and controlled.

By the turn of the twentieth century, however, the immigrant influx of the prior half-century had altered the reality of the cities. As the Boston Brahmin Henry Adams wrote in his autobiography: "The old universe was thrown into the ash heap and a new one created." The order of things—what Adams called "restraint, law and unity"—had been changed forever. The old stock remained socially dominant, but they kept apart from the new arrivals as aristocracies had decided to do around the world.

Their dreams of an easy assimilation of immigrants under the enlightened and benign leadership of a select group of elite families gave way to the reality that immigrants would continue to disturb the settled fabric of society. They would not, and could not, conform to upper-class norms. Even the new technology proved unnerving: "Prosperity never before imagined, power never yet wielded by man, speed never reached by anything but a meteor, had made the world irritable, nervous, querulous, unreasonable and afraid," said Adams.

The productivity of the new manufacturing economy produced numerous consequences. Gradually, some immigrants and their progeny moved out of rank poverty into the working class. President James Garfield once said that the struggle of the human race was divided into two chapters—the struggle to acquire leisure and the struggle to know what to do with it. Without the habits and pretensions of the aristocracy, immigrant families sought pastimes for their enjoyment.

There was at least one—and perhaps only one—circumstance where dominant and subordinate groups, new and old immigrants divided by social class and religion, could come together if not as equals, then at least as co-participants. The cheers of all were of equal weight at the baseball park. Religion divided, while baseball united. As Annie Savoy said in the movie *Bull Durham:* "I believe in the Church of Baseball. I've tried all the major religions and most of the minor ones. And the only church that truly feeds the soul, day-in day-out, is the Church of Baseball."

Although segregated within the stadium by class—the menu of ticket prices ensured that—all spectators could claim equal "ownership" in this one enterprise. Unlike sporting clubs with restricted memberships, the park was open to all with the price of admission. And the parks were a welcome refuge of green amidst cities of gray and brown, smoke and noise.

The players on the field at the Huntington Avenue Grounds wore "BOSTON" on the front of their uniforms, a source of great community pride. The Boston ballplayers were known as Collins's boys, after Irishman Jimmy Collins, their stalwart captain and manager who hailed from industrial Buffalo.

The baseball club belonged to the Irish, the Jews, the Yankees, and the Brahmins—to the entire city. As the former New York Yankees president Michael Burke said: "A baseball club is part of the chemistry of the city. A game isn't just an athletic contest. It's a picnic, a kind of town meeting."

Baseball drew together immigrants of many generations, but certainly not every person. Many were too busy working twelve hours a day, seven days a week, to keep their families fed and housed to waste attention on recreation and amusement. Others found the baseball game experience too noisy and unwieldy. The game was everywhere, however, played by children within their segregated neighborhoods; young adults in social, work, and church groups; and a few extremely talented professionals at the ballpark. Most could identify with, cheer for, and claim ownership in the local nine. As a popular song of the era said:

> *The men who lead the world today in all athletic games*
> *Are brawny sons of Uncle Sam, with good old Yankee names.*
> *Brady and O'Toole, Dooin and McColl*
> *McInemy and McBarney, Harrigan, McVey and Kearney . . .*
> *Connie Mack and John McGraw—all together shout Hurrah! . . .*
> *There's Rosenheimer, Jacobs, Weiner, Gimble, Sax and Straus*
> *They're all good American names!*

Professional baseball did not transform immigrants into Americans. For some, however, baseball did represent the mythic values of America, probably as accurately as the aphorism that the streets in this new country were paved with gold. Professor Ted White has written that a "remarkable synergy existed between the game of baseball and the aspiration of Americans in the first two decades of the twentieth century."

We should be careful, however, not to allow exuberance to outpace the facts. Baseball was only a diversion, although a very important one in the lives of many. Boston rooter Jacob C. Morse wrote in a column for the *Pittsburgh Press* on the morning of the fourth game of the World Series:

> The man is not entirely All-American today who isn't up on baseball. There is something lacking. Baseball is today a firmly fixed institution, and it is waxing warmer each year.

The professional game did offer a rare opportunity for the disparate groups who had immigrated to this country to meet in one place at one time and root in unison for a common goal—victory in a contest against a club representing another city. It was, as Professor White maintains, a source of great civic pride—not ethnic or religious pride, but a secular pride of place. It was an enormously valuable experience for those who had come from so many different cultures and who lived their lives in America separated from their fellow immigrants of different origins. They could never connect to the founders of the country, but they could identify with their hometown nine. As Frank Deford has explained, by the end of the nineteenth century "baseball was developing as a kind of adhesive that held together the evolving modern city and all its diverse types." *Scribner's* magazine wrote: "Baseball united all classes and conditions of men from the White House through every person of our cosmopolitan population."

The more significant social, political, and economic questions involving the deluge of immigrants were not settled by the simple pastime of baseball. How would Americans of the twentieth century form a sufficient consensus to address internal and external economic and social problems? Would the country empower all its citizens—women, blacks, and new immigrants—in an effort to realize the promises of its founders? How would the vast disparities in wealth and opportunity be addressed, if at all? None of these important matters were settled at ballparks; after all, baseball was only a game.

HUNTINGTON AVENUE GROUNDS

*An estimated crowd of 25,000 fanatics attended
the third game of the first World Series at the
Huntington Avenue Grounds. At 2:00 P.M., an hour
before the start of the contest, the outfield ropes
gave way before the surging crowd. Fans stampeded
toward the diamond, intent on watching their
heroes toss the ball around in infield practice.*

1

The Huntington Avenue Grounds: A Commoner Event

> I see great things in baseball. It's our game — the American game. It will take our people out of doors, fill them with oxygen, give them a larger physical stoicism. Tend to relieve us from being a nervous, dyspeptic set. Repair these losses, and be a blessing to us.
>
> —Walt Whitman

The crowds began arriving at the wooden gates by 1:00 P.M., two hours before game time. They had come to witness the first game of the first World Series, and newspapers had cautioned patrons to arrive early if they were to attend "what is expected to be the greatest series in the history of baseball." It was October 1, 1903, a mild but cloudy early fall day in Boston.

The first World Series was the brainchild of the owner of the National League Pittsburgh club, Barney Dreyfuss, a German-Jewish immigrant, referred to by the Pittsburgh newspapers as the "little magnate." The 1903 regular season produced two runaway victors, Dreyfuss's mighty Pirates of Pittsburgh, who had captured their third straight National League title, and the Boston club of the upstart American League. (The ten Boston newspapers referred to the local nine as the Boston "Americans" or occasionally as the "Pilgrims." The team would not receive its hosiery nickname, the "Red Sox," until 1907.) Boston newspapers heralded a "great struggle" with the leagues' champions "meet[ing] for blood." The *Pittsburgh Press* sporting page reported: "The enthusiasm is greater than has ever before been seen in this city." Boston was "baseball mad."

The electric trolley cars disgorged their human contents along crowded Huntington Avenue about a half-mile west of Copley Square. On the north side of the thoroughfare stood Boston's magnificent three-year-old Symphony Hall. On the south side stood the left-field wall of the Huntington Ave-nue Grounds, the huge wooden edifice that beckoned the throng that day. Erected only three years earlier as the first home of the Boston Americans, the Grounds had been consecrated by Cy Young with his first American League win on April 30, 1901. The playing field was expansive: left field measured 350 feet down the line, right field a mere 280, and no one had ever accurately measured center field, but it was estimated at an impressive 530 feet from home plate. Located on the trolley car line on the border of Boston and Roxbury's Mission Hill, the new park was easily reached by the urban populous.

The Boston Americans were not the Hub's only professional club. The National League entry, called the Beaneaters, occupied a nearby facil-ity, the South End Grounds. To attract fans to cross over the New York, New Haven, and Hartford Railroad tracks from the South End and desert the National League Beaneaters, Charles Somers, the first owner of the American League franchise in Boston, set admission at half the price of a National League game. He also signed a team of strong, experienced major leaguers, many well-known "artistes" from the roster of the Beaneaters. By 1903, the public's affection had switched to the American League team, led by the acclaimed captain Jimmy Collins.

The 1903 National League champions, the Pittsburgh Pirates, arrived the day before the Series opener from western Pennsylvania, accompanied by their rooters, who "expressed the utmost confidence" in the outcome of the best-of-nine Series. The club played an exhibition game in Buffalo on its way east, a common event at the turn of the century and a way for the players to earn a little extra money. (They trounced the Eastern League club 9–1.) During their stay in the Hub, the Pirates and their followers, including many gamblers, boarded at the Vendome Hotel on the corner of Commonwealth Avenue and Dartmouth Street in the Back Bay. Most of the Boston players stayed at the Putnam Hotel ("Puts") on Huntington Avenue. A few blocks away, between the Fens and Massachusetts Avenue, the ladies of Boston's red-light district did a flourishing business.

The *Boston Post* reported that Bostonians were ready for the match: "Interest all over the city and by all classes is at fever heat. In the downtown hotels and sporting resorts [betting parlors] last evening nothing else was talked of." Boston's general manager, Joe Smart, had doubled admission prices for the occasion. Spectators paid 50¢ for bleacher seats and standing room and $1 for grandstand seats. Many of those in attendance had played baseball in their youth and remained avid followers of the game.

By 2:00 P.M., the nine thousand bench seats down both foul lines were taken, but the crowds continued to arrive in waves from the trolley cars. Men sat on every available inch of the twelve-foot fence that surrounded the outfield. "Thousands and thousands filed down the little avenue to the entrances and went their separate ways as determined by their desires and their purses," reported the *Boston Herald*. More than sixteen thousand "wildly enthusiastic" fans, almost all male, attended that day's festivities, thousands ringing the outfield behind ropes, the largest crowd ever to see a baseball game in Boston. A "small army of policemen" kept order in the good-natured crowd. The *Boston Post* reported that "Everybody seemed to be at the game. Business men rubbed shoulders with their clerks, and City Hall 'pols' and their heelers were on an equal footing. Like a Harvard–Yale football game, almost everyone of any importance was to be seen." The *Boston Herald* echoed this chorus: "Side by side sat clerks, ministers and sports [gamblers], college professors and graduates of the sand lots, all bound together by one great all-absorbing love for the national game." It was a rare commoner event where virtually all of Boston cheered together to achieve the same goal.

The People of Boston

Representatives of all segments of the Boston populous enthusiastically embraced their sports heroes. The Royal Rooters, a contingent of Irish men dressed in their Sunday finest (including the new "Continental Special" bowler hat that could be purchased for only $2), were the greatest baseball fanatics. They occupied reserved bleacher seats at the Huntington Avenue Grounds behind first base. Rooter Charley Lavis was the "master of ceremonies." Lavis, John Fitzgerald, and "Nuf Ced" Mike McGreevey, whose Third Base Saloon the Boston Rooters patronized before and after the contests, led the Rooters in songs and cheers.

Prizefighter James J. Corbett took his front-row seat among the Boston rooters, and local hero John L. Sullivan, the "Boston Strong Boy," sat on the Boston players' bench chatting with manager Jimmy Collins before the game began. Born in 1858, in the Roxbury section of Boston, Sullivan was a gifted baseball player in his youth and was offered a contract to play for the Cincinnati Red Stockings. Instead he chose to pursue his fortune in the ring, and he became the most celebrated boxer of the nineteenth century, America's first sports superstar. On June 26, 1880, Sullivan announced that he would fight anyone in America, with or without gloves, for $500. In 1892, Sullivan met his match when Jim Corbett won the heavyweight crown by knocking out Sullivan in the twenty-first round of their historic match in New Orleans. That was the "Great John L's" last fight, ending his fabled career with thirty-seven wins and one loss. Corbett held the heavyweight title from 1892 until 1897 and had fought his last fight on August 14, 1903, against champion James Jeffries.

Former Massachusetts governor Winthrop Murray Crane, who had served three one-year terms starting in 1899, was also in attendance that day. A member of a wealthy and paternalistic Dalton, Massachusetts, family, he managed the family's stock portfolio and philanthropic activities before entering politics. In addition to the churches, hospitals, and temperance organizations that received his gifts, Crane contributed substantial amounts to the Republican Party. He gained nationwide notice in 1902 when as governor he mediated a crippling teamsters strike in the Bay State. In 1904,

Crane was rewarded by the Massachusetts legislature (the "Great and General Court," as it was called) with appointment to the U. S. Senate, where he served as a staunch member of the Republican old guard.

William Henry Moody, secretary of the navy during Teddy Roosevelt's administration, also came to enjoy the day's baseball festivities. He was born in his family's two-hundred-year-old home in Newbury, Massachusetts, a town his Puritan ancestor and namesake, William Moody of Suffolk, England, had founded in 1635. A graduate of the Phillips Academy and Harvard University—where he had played catcher and captained the baseball teams—the Brahmin Moody was a devoted "baseball crank," an inveterate fanatic of the game. He served three terms in Congress before accepting an appointment to the Roosevelt Cabinet. As attorney general in 1904, he would regularly attend the baseball contests played by the Washington Nationals in the nation's capital, cheering on their stalwart hurler Walter Johnson. In 1906, President Roosevelt appointed Moody to the U.S. Supreme Court.

John I. Taylor, son of General Charles Taylor, the patrician owner of the *Boston Globe*, took his regular seat behind home plate. Taylor would play a critical role in Boston baseball history. In 1904, he would become the owner of the Boston club, which he renamed the Red Sox in 1907, and, using his father's money, built a new concrete stadium for his club. Fenway Park would open in 1912.

John Roberts Tunis, the fourteen-year-old son of a Brahmin Unitarian minister, also attended the first World Series. Later, after graduating from Harvard and studying law, Tunis became a celebrated writer of sports books for children and frequently contributed to the *Atlantic Monthly, Collier's, Harper's* and the *New Yorker.* In his autobiography, *A Measure of Independence,* Tunis recalled standing in line to enter the Huntington Avenue Grounds and hearing the music from the approaching cavalcade. The Royal Rooters, dressed in their finest black suits and high white collars, each with "his ticket stuck jauntily in the hatband of his derby," strutted into the Grounds led by "Nuf Ced" McGreevey.

Politicians attending the Democratic State Convention skipped the afternoon session to attend the sporting festivities and joined with Republicans in supporting the local nine. Boston mayor Patrick A. Collins could not attend. The city's street commissioner, James A. Galvin, presented Boston's captain, Jimmy Collins, with a note from the mayor:

> Baseball Team
> Huntington Avenue Grounds
>
> Dear Sir—In a contest between Boston and any other city for supremacy, either in the domain of brain or brawn, the sympathies and best wishes of our citizens are always with Boston champions.
>   In this spirit and interpreting the popular desire, I sincerely hope that your brave corps of ball players will triumph over the invading forces of Pittsburgh, as they have triumphed over all their opponents during the season.

Some of Boston's loyal fans were not in attendance for that first game but would attend later contests. Many German and Russian Jews, among Boston's newest immigrant groups, were otherwise occupied on October 1, 1903. It was Yom Kippur, the holiest day of the Jewish year. However, led by Rabbi Charles Fleischer, the distinguished patriarch of one of Boston's oldest congregations, Temple Adeth Israel, they would be present for the second game. Rabbi Fleischer viewed the game as the guest of President Dreyfuss and his Pittsburgh rabbi, who had made the trip east with the Pirates owner. Five years later, in a widely read article in *Baseball Magazine,* Rabbi Fleischer would extol the virtues of baseball and his personal love for the game.

The Athens of America

By the early 1820s, Boston had become known as the "Athens of America," a romantic vision of the city that Ralph Waldo Emerson helped spread when he wrote:

> This town of Boston has a history. It is not an accident, not a windmill, or a railroad station, or cross-roads tavern, or an army-barracks grown up by time and luck to a place of wealth; but a seat of humanity, of men of principle, obeying a sentiment and marching loyally whither that should lead them; so that its annals are great historical lines, inextricably national; part of the history of political liberty. I do not speak with any fondness, but the language of coldest history, when I say that Boston commands attention as the town which was appointed in the destiny of nations to lead the civilization of North America.

Emerson's rhapsody was based partly on fact, but mostly on fancy. Emerson downplayed the impact of the new immigrants who had settled on Boston's Shawmut Peninsula. He also ignored the streak of arrogance that characterized upper-class Bostonians. A reporter for the *Pittsburgh Dispatch* wrote: "Massachusetts boasts a long line of distinguished sons and daughters, whose greatness is hammered into the average American who chanced to be born elsewhere, from paregoric to the shroud."

Boston at the turn of the twentieth century had 560,000 inhabitants, making it the nation's fifth largest metropolis. In many ways, it was typical of American coastal cities. It was a city of immigrants, some recent, others native to these shores for generations, but still emotionally tied to their ancestral homelands. Boston was a city of ethnic enclaves, each with its own churches and markets, civic organizations and sporting groups. The city's multitudes had few experiences in common, but one they did share was an interest as spectators and participants in the national game of baseball.

Boston's economy was booming in the first decade of the twentieth century, and it was a good time to be rich. Boston was a major international financial center, and its financiers supplied the capital that fueled the industrial age. America had transformed itself into a world economic power, and Boston was an important player in that transformation. The large industrial towns north of Boston—Lowell, Lawrence, and Haverhill—manufactured goods for a world market accessed through the piers of Boston's harbor.

Emerson had also written glowingly of Boston's power to level and assimi-late disparate social groups, but this too was wistful fiction. Boston at the turn of the century was a decidedly class society. Members of the privileged Brah-min upper class, the "Proper Bostonians," ruled the social scene from their perch on Beacon Hill. In the 1880s and 1890s, some had moved into newly constructed brownstone mansions in the Back Bay, built on land claimed from the Charles River. Others had begun the exodus to the nearby suburbs such as Brookline, said to be the wealthiest town in America at the time.

Although the upper class had once controlled Boston's civic and public institutions, by the turn of the twentieth century it had lost its dominance in political matters to the American-born offspring of Irish immigrants. The Irish had flocked to Boston to escape the devastating potato famine of the late 1840s. Segregated in the poorest neighborhoods and clustered into Catholic parishes, the Irish saw America as a temporary haven, a way station back to the home country once conditions allowed. Meanwhile, Irish men provided muscle power for industry, and Irish women worked in the homes of wealthy Bostonians.

By the 1880s and 1890s, however, the "return to Eire" had lost its talis-manic effect on the immigrants. The Irish community had successfully mar-shaled its political strength and wrested control of the governmental machin-ery of the region (and the abundant employment opportunities it offered) from the Brahmins and the Yankees. The Irish were in Boston to stay.

The century's last wave of immigrants brought masses from eastern and southern Europe to the Hub in the 1880s and 1890s. Jews had emigrated from Germany earlier in the century, and their small number and citified backgrounds facilitated assimilation into the Boston mix. But the Russian and Polish Jews, escaping from governmental and religious persecution, were not so easily absorbed. Together with southern Italians as well as Greeks, Hun-garians, Romanians, and other Slavic immigrants, they added further com-plexity to the demographic landscape. Like the Irish, these newcomers were subject to discrimination in housing and employment. Unlike the Irish, they were yet to establish roots in the New World. America was a confusing place. How could these disparate elements ever form a common community?

The patrician senator from Massachusetts, Henry Cabot Lodge, warned that these masses of new immigrants threatened "the very fabric of the Anglo-American race." He worried publicly about the dilution of the "American stock." His rival in Massachusetts politics was congressman (and baseball enthusiast) John F. Fitzgerald, "Honey Fitz," who would later serve the city as mayor. (His grandson, John Fitzgerald Kennedy, would serve the nation as president.) Fitzgerald responded to Lodge's gauntlet. These immigrants, he said, have "as much right as your father or mine," because, after all, "it was only a difference of a few ships" between their arrival in Boston. Lodge's battle to impose limits on immigration would consume his attention for decades.

Boston's African American population remained small in number and marginalized in society. Other immigrant groups took solace in the fact that even if their economic and living conditions were dreadful, blacks enjoyed even less favor and opportunity. At the turn of the twentieth century, there were African Americans of great accomplishment, such as W. E. B. Dubois, a western Massachusetts native. Dubois had more important work to do. He wrote in his autobiography, "I could not waste my time on baseball." In 1903, in *The Souls of Black Folks,* Dubois recorded that blacks remained "serfs bound to the soil." He accurately reported that "The problem of the twentieth century is the problem of the color line, the question as to how far differences of race . . . are going to be made . . . the basis of denying to half the world . . . the opportunities of modern civilization." In Boston, blacks would remain invisible and excluded. It would take almost five decades before African Americans could participate as players on major league clubs.

Life in Boston

By 1903, Americans were enjoying the fruits of a rapid and unprecedented technological revolution. Alfred Russel Wallace, in an essay entitled *The Wonderful Century,* listed the most remarkable achievements of the nineteenth century, inventions that were "perfectly new departures, and which have so rapidly developed as to have profoundly affected many of our habits, and even our thoughts and our language":

1. Railways, which have revolutionized land travel and the distribution of commodities.

2. Steam Navigation, which has done the same thing for ocean travel, and has besides led to the entire reconstruction of the navies of the world.

3. Electric Telegraphs, which have produced an even greater revolution in the communication of thought.

4. The Telephone, which transmits, or rather reproduces, the voice of the speaker at a distance.

5. Friction Matches, which have revolutionized the modes of obtaining fire.

6. Gas-lighting, which enormously improved outdoor and other illumination.

7. Electric-lighting, another advance now threatening to supersede gas.

8. Photography, an art which is to the external forms of Nature what printing is to thought.

9. The Phonograph, which preserves and reproduces sounds as photography preserves and reproduces forms.

10. The Roentgen Rays, which render many opaque objects transparent, and open up a new world to photography.

11. Spectrum Analysis, which so greatly extends our knowledge of the universe that by its assistance we are able to ascertain the relative heat and chemical constitution of the stars, and ascertain the existence, and measure the rate of motion, of stellar bodies which are entirely invisible.

12. The use of Anesthetics, rendering the most severe surgical operations painless.

13. The use of Antiseptics in surgical operations, which has still further extended the means of saving life.

Advances in the use of electricity and developments in mechanized transportation transformed daily life. Electric lights had replaced kerosene lamps in many homes, but coal remained the primary source of heat.

People were no longer bound to their neighborhoods. Affordable public trolley and transit systems — the omnibus and horse-drawn streetcars, later replaced by electric-powered streetcars—allowed Bostonians to venture into new geographic areas in pursuit of work and pleasure. Most people in Boston, however, worked close to their homes, and many toiled in their homes performing piecework for menial wages.

America's railroads freed the new middle class to travel on the same trains (if not in the same cars) as their social betters. For the wealthy, their chauffeur-driven new electric automobiles, the "broughams," could speed along at twenty-five miles per hour, but most still relied on their own horse and carriage. Just before the turn of the century, Boston had built the nation's first subway, although when it opened in 1898 it extended only from Scollay Square to Arlington Street, less than a mile in length. Where the subway ended, trolley cars plied Boston's streets, first pulled by horses and later powered by electricity.

For the very wealthy, whom Mark DeWolfe Howe called the "cultured, moral and conservative" members of "Boston Proper," it was a time of excess. Attended to by Irish maids, cooks, butlers, and assorted other servants, the Brahmins enjoyed their wealth and their status in an America that enjoyed good times. Brahmin families would travel to the Continent each year accompanied by an entourage of servants. Their Beacon Hill and Back Bay mansions were lit by electricity and heated by steam. Their homes included elevators, bathtubs with hot and cold running water, and telephones. Outside, their peaceful streets were brightly lit at night by electric lights. Nearby, the luxurious new Hotel Lenox on the corner of Boylston and Exeter Streets in Back Bay offered travelers first-class accommodations.

The poor of Boston did not share in the good life. Crowded into unsanitary housing, their part of the city was congested, dirty, and noisy. For the Irish, the Catholic Church served as the anchor to their tradition and the way of life they had left in Ireland. The Church also held out the prospect of eternal salvation and redemption for enduring difficult earthly circumstances. The religious sanctuary was the one physical place in which an immigrant could escape the grime and noise of the slum. The church building was a refuge—silent, clean, spacious, and free of odors.

Boston in the early 1900s was not Eden. Neither the rich nor the poor could escape illness. Although medicine had made enormous strides, immunization against childhood diseases was not yet available. Children were often ill. Typhoid, measles, scarlet fever, diphtheria, and tuberculosis contributed to the high death rate among children of all social classes. Medical care remained primitive, and communicable diseases would rampage through a community. Smallpox was a dreaded contagion, and infant mortality remained high.

It was generally believed that activity in the fresh air was the best defense against contagion and delinquency. The nation's first playground was built in Boston in 1885, and immigrant children learned how to play baseball at local settlement houses. Frederick Law Olmsted, a Brahmin famous for designing Central Park in New York, came home to Boston and put baseball diamonds throughout his Emerald Necklace of public parks from Boston Common to Franklin Park in Dorchester. Ball games had been played on the Common for decades, and snowball fights in winter proved a healthy recreation. Even attendance at a sporting event was seen as a wholesome endeavor, though drinking was rampant and diseases were communicated by the close contact, especially in a stadium bursting with crowds.

Although the 1903 World Series was an important marker in the development of spectator sports in Boston, it was certainly not the first time bat met ball on the Shawmut Peninsula. James D'Wolfe Lovett, a great amateur baseball player from the mid-nineteenth-century Olympics Club of Boston, related the story of the December 1869 political effort by baseball enthusiasts to preserve the right to play ball on Boston Common. They ran a "base ball ticket" of candidates committed to protecting their recreational opportunities, and they prevailed at the polls. Lovett extolled baseball as "a good healthy recreation, calling for recruits who must be sound mentally and physically." On the other hand, Lovett objected to the gloves that players took to wearing as the nineteenth century progressed, referring to them as a "mitten, . . . a padded contrivance."

By the turn of the twentieth century, many on the teeming urban landscape sought entertainment opportunities that were within their financial means and physical reach. Leisure time, a new concept, was available even to members of the working class after their daily factory shift. Neighborhood saloons offered men a social environment among their own folk, and the new, affordable public transportation system offered mobility beyond the walking neighborhood. Music halls provided entertainment appealing to all but those with the most refined tastes. Spectator sports also served as a universal attraction. Harvard football played by the sons of scions captured media attention, but few among the masses could identify with the Crimson eleven. The greatest attraction was the national pastime, the game of professional baseball, which drew crowds each afternoon except Sunday to the ballpark. (Blue laws prohibited entertainment on the Sabbath.) The World Series of 1903 would prove a great attraction for all classes of Bostonians.

The Rival Clubs

On paper, the rivals in the 1903 World Series seemed fairly matched, although most neutral observers favored the experienced Pirates. One local follower of the game said to a reporter for the hometown *Boston Post:* "You may as well toss up a penny and pick the winner as to try to figure out which team should win." Each club had its enthusiasts, and all spectators looked forward to the spirited contests. The *Pittsburgh Press* remarked: "If confidence would win games, the opening contest would certainly result in a tie."

The veteran Pittsburgh club had won its third pennant of the new century, powered by strong hitting and steady pitching. In 1903, the Pirates won ninety-one games and lost only forty-nine, six games ahead of its nearest rival, John McGraw's New York Giants. The club's nickname, the Pirates, was affixed in 1891 when the Philadelphia Athletics of the American Association failed to sign their star infielder, Louis Bierbauer. The second baseman jumped to the Pittsburgh club of the National League. The Athletics protested Pittsburgh's action, labeling the club "pirates" for stealing Bierbauer. Pittsburgh newspapers and the club's faithful fanatics proudly adopted the moniker.

First among the Pirate stars was the great shortstop Honus Wagner, generally referred to as "Hans" or "the Flying Dutchman." In 1903, Wagner led the National League in batting with a .355 average and in triples with 19. The *Pittsburgh Press* called him the team's "bright particular star," and the *Pittsburgh Gazette* said he was the "boss batter" of the National League. The other Pirate players complemented Wagner's productive hitting and prodigious fielding.

The well-liked player-manager Fred Clarke covered left field, a role he would play for nineteen of his twenty-one major league seasons. He began his major league career with Louisville in 1894 and hit 5 for 5 in his first game, the only player ever to do so. He continued to post stellar statistics for his entire Hall of Fame career, batting .321 with 2,672 career hits and 1,602 managerial wins. Center fielder Clarence Howeth "Ginger" Beaumont, the speedy leadoff man, had been the 1902 National League batting champion with a .357 average and led the 1903 Pirates in runs, hits, games played, and at bats. Completing the star-studded outfield, Jimmy Sebring played right field. Surrounding Wagner in the infield were the diminutive Tommy Leach at third and Claude Richey at second. The 200-pound William Bransfield, called "Kitty" because of his feminine hairstyle, anchored first. Eddie Phelps caught most of the games that season for the Pittsburgh club.

This Pittsburgh squad was known, as the *Boston Post* reported, to be "one of the speediest teams in the game. With a man on first a base hit will in almost every case put him on third." If Boston was to prevail, it would have to counteract Pittsburgh's hit-and-run game.

The Pirates had started the season with a powerful pitching staff, and they did not fail to meet expectations. Charles Phillippe (24–7), referred to as "Deacon" because of his sterling character, and Sam Leever (25–7), the "Goshen Schoolmaster" (named after his hometown in Ohio), had both logged stellar seasons. Phillippe would bear most of the work from the mound during the 1903 Series. Even before the first match, Captain Clarke told the *Pittsburgh Gazette* that the Deacon was in the finest shape, and "the way he cuts loose with his bender is a caution." Leever had led the National League with a 2.06 earned run average, but by season's end his arm was tiring, and he had hurt his shoulder trapshooting in a tournament in Charleroi, Pennsylvania. Leever turned to a Youngstown chiropractor named John "Bonesetter" Reese, who was paid $500 by club owner Barney Dreyfuss to assist club trainer Ed Laforce during the games played in Boston. Although the Bonesetter was ill-equipped to provide any real treatment—he was a former steelworker and oil driller who used a combination of massage and mysticism—the Pirates players thought he was "the greatest man in the business."

Pittsburgh's third starter, Ed Doheny (16–8), had been overcome by paranoid delusions as the season neared its end. On the evening of September 21, Doheny left Pittsburgh in the company of his clergyman brother, who escorted him home to Andover, Massachusetts, just north of Boston. He would never play baseball again. William Park "Brickyard" Kennedy (9–6) was in the last year of a thirteen-year major league career, all but two campaigns with the Brooklyn Bridegrooms (also known to the locals as the Trolley Dodgers, later shortened to the familiar Dodgers). Two little-used rookies, Bucky Veil (5–3) and Gus Thompson (2–2), completed the staff. All in all, the Pirates were a tough and seasoned club.

The Boston Americans carried fourteen players on their roster during the 1903 season, including five pitchers and one little-used utility fielder. The starting eight field players played almost every game. Led by the immensely popular Jimmy Collins, who served as the field manager, captain, and star third baseman, the club attracted widespread interest among the Boston fanatics, especially from the city's strong Irish contingent. In its history of the members of a champion team published two days before the first game of the World Series, the *Boston Herald* wrote of Collins with hometown hyperbole: "His record with the Boston Nationals and Americans is so well known that any discussion on this point is superfluous." The *Boston Post* wrote: "Much of the American League's popularity in this city belongs to Collins. . . . His players swear by him." Known for his modesty, this Irish son of a Buffalo police captain was the leading personality on the pennant-winning club. Jacob C. Morse, the *Boston Herald'* s baseball expert, said the inhabitants of the bleachers of this country would elect Collins "the supreme 'it' of the baseball fraternity. . . . The secret of it is that Jim Collins is just chock full of baseball."

The Americans' first baseman was George "Candy" Lachance. A native of Waterbury, Connecticut, this dour veteran of ten years in the majors had joined the Boston club in 1902. "Though anything but a showy player," according to the *Herald,* Lachance was "a wonder in fielding bad throws . . . and is sure on fly balls." Albert "Hobe" Ferris, from Providence, Rhode Island, "the fastest thrower in the league," played second base. The 1903 season was a career year at shortstop for little Freddy Parent—a native of Biddeford, Maine, and of French-Canadian descent—who batted .304 with 80 RBI.

In Boston's outfield, the powerful Patrick Henry "Patsy" Dougherty played left. Dougherty led the American League in runs and hits and batted .331 for the 1903 campaign to lead all Boston batters, ranking third in the circuit after Cleveland's Larry Lajoie (.344) and Detroit's Sam Crawford (.335). Charles "Chick" Stahl patrolled the broad reaches of center field. John "Buck" Freeman, a 170-pound power hitter who led the American League in 1903 with 13 home runs and 104 RBI, played right field.

The Boston pitching staff was led by the formidable thirty-four-year-old hurler Cy Young (28–9), who had led the American League that season with 34 complete games, 7 shutouts, and 341⅔ innings pitched while batting .321. During the 1903 campaign, Young had surpassed Pud Galvin's record (361) for the most victories in baseball history. He finished the year with 379 wins and would complete his career eight years later with the insurmountable record of 511 victories. Bill Dineen (21–13), whose name was sometimes spelled "Dinneen," would prove to be the Series' hero for the Boston nine. Thomas James "Long Tom" Hughes (20–7), afflicted with a sore arm at season's end, completed the starting rotation. Cy Young's pal, the light-hitting Lou Criger—"the greatest catcher living," according to the *Boston Herald*—caught most of the games for Boston. He was lauded in the *Pittsburgh Press* for his "marvelous throwing to the pillows." Criger posed a significant threat to the Pirates' base stealing.

This then would be the match-up: The three-time National League pennant-winning club led by Honus Wagner's hitting and fielding against the upstart American League's champions from Boston with veteran pitching from Cy Young and Bill Dineen. The *Pittsburgh Dispatch* puffed that "Boston will get the beating of a lifetime. . . . Just watch us go!" Most observers, however, thought one club or the other would not easily win the Series, and they were prescient. It would be, as the *Boston Post* had predicted, "a battle royal." "These things can never be properly told, but they will go down in history with the spectators who heard and saw them," wrote the *Boston Herald*.

The Contest Commences

Each club supplied one umpire for the game—Hank O'Day by the National Leaguers and Tommy Connolly by the American—and both were subject to the approval of the opposition. The two men would umpire the entire Series, taking turns behind the plate. Captains Collins and Clarke agreed to a ground rule that awarded a batter a triple for any ball hit into the roped-off crowd standing in the outfield. Boston's megaphone man, Charles Moore, announced the lineups to all parts of the field, and the appointed time had arrived. A gong sounded, and Umpire Connolly barked, "Play." Cy Young took the mound for the Boston squad.

Young quickly dispatched Beaumont on a fly to center and then Clarke, who fouled out to the catcher. Then, with two outs, the Pirates erupted for four runs on three Boston errors that would ensure the National League club's victory in the opening contest. Third baseman Tommy Leach, who had earlier been reported as ill with a "small eruption on the back of one finger," flied deep to right. The ball fell among the roped-off crowd, giving him a ground-rule triple. Wagner lined a single over the shortstop's head, driving Leach home. The Flying Dutchman then stole second, moved to third on Ferris's error on Bransfield's grounder, and came home on a delayed double steal when Criger threw the ball over Freddy Parent's head into center field. Staggered by the sloppy play of his teammates, "old dependable Cy" was not able to "stem the tide." Ritchey walked and Sebring, the hitting star of the day, tallied Bransfield and Ritchey on a single to left, the first of three safeties for the right fielder, including an inside-the-park home run to the far reaches of center field in the seventh inning. The hometown team seemed to observers to be nervous at the start, and the previously boisterous Boston crowd "sat in silence." The Pirates faithful, who had made the trip east to root for "their favorite buccaneers long and loud," said the *Pittsburgh Press,* were enjoying the festivities fully.

Deacon Phillippe was masterful on the mound for the Pirates "from first to last like the artist that he is," said the *Pittsburgh Press.* The *Boston Post* reported: "To Phillippe mainly belongs the credit of Pittsburgh's victory." He was "the Whole Cheese." Boston went 1–2–3 the first three innings—five of the first seven batters struck out—and did not score until the bottom of the seventh, by which time Pittsburgh had taken an insurmountable 7–0 lead. Phillippe pitched "a game that the locals simply could not fathom." His "high drop ball and a wide out curve that swept continually beyond the reach of the longest bat kept Captain Collins's men stretching their necks and shoulders . . . in a vain effort to connect."

Both pitchers hurled complete games, the norm in 1903, but Phillippe won the day, aided by some "terrific batting," said the *Pittsburgh Gazette,* that "completely outclassed the Boston Americans at all points." The *Boston Globe* opined, "it's not often that Uncle Cyrus fails to land the money, even if he is a bit fat." (He was well over 200 pounds by his mid-thirties.) Young would redeem himself before the Series was completed, however. The final score that first day was 7–3, a propitious beginning for the National League entry in a game that took less than two hours to complete. The American League team appeared unsettled and uncertain in their play. In particular, its usually reliable catcher, Lou Criger, seemed unsteady with two throwing errors. (The *Pittsburgh Press* reported that Criger was so upset by his performance that "he used language unfit for publication." The *Pittsburgh Gazette* characterized his poor performance as the result of "stage fright.") The orderly crowd, which had stayed until the end of the contest, "took defeat quietly," and "the loyalty of the Boston rooters never wavered." The *Pittsburgh Gazette* reported that the Boston faithful were in "sackcloth and ashes," while the Pirates' supporters "were jubilant and kept the sedate old town in a whirl of excitement by their celebration."

GAME 1

Team	1	2	3	4	5	6	7	8	9	R	H	E
Pittsburgh	4	0	1	1	0	0	1	0	0	7	6	2
Boston	0	0	0	0	0	0	2	0	1	3	6	4

Some newspaper accounts questioned whether Boston lost the game on purpose. Because the players were to be paid out of total receipts for the entire Series, they would benefit financially if more games were played. The local "sports," as the gamblers were called, lost money, having given odds on a Boston victory. Some $50,000 was wagered on the first game's outcome. "The big crowd, particularly in the third base pavilion, was gambling crazy." (No one seemed to remember that on August 17, 1903, American League president, Ban Johnson, had prohibited betting at all American League parks.)

That night, after dinner at Back Bay's Vendome Hotel, the Pittsburgh players went to Keith's Theatre, where they were said to have "enjoyed the performance immensely." The Boston nine saw the performance at the Grand Opera House. Barney Dreyfuss and the other Pittsburgh club officials took in the *Yankee Consul* show at the Tremont Theatre, advertised as "a new comic opera in two acts" by Henry M. Blossom, Jr., and Alfred G. Robyn. (The next year, the show would open on Broadway, one of many hits Blossom and Robyn would enjoy.) The visitors made plans to see John C. Fisher's *The Silver Slipper* at the Colonial Theatre after the second game of the World Series.

The Tradition

The first game of the first World Series began a tradition that would last with little change for a century. Each October, the attention of America's sports fans turns to two ballparks where the winners of the league pennants battle for the hyperbolic title of Champions of the World. (For most of the century, the "world" stretched only from Boston to St. Louis across the northern tier of American states.)

Those fans who attended on the occasion of the first game came from all of Boston's communities. They were day laborers, Yankee craftsmen, Irish factory workers, and Brahmins—first-, second-, and third-generation immigrants—but their lives were so different from one another that baseball was the only event they would share in common. For the century to come, Americans from every social class and ethnic identity would join in celebration of the national game.

BAN JOHNSON

Ban Johnson, the thirty-six-year-old driven, overweight moose of a man, whose single-mindedness and egotism would not countenance failure, converted a regional minor circuit into a major league by stealing the finest stars of the National League. By January 1903, the magnates of the National League sued for peace.

2

The National Game: Constructing the Pastime

George Wright was one of many sports heroes in attendance that October afternoon when the World Series began in Boston, and his many fans gave him a hearty welcome. Wright was the nation's finest baseball player during the formative years of the professional game in the 1860s and 1870s. By 1903, the fifty-six-year-old Wright served as Boston's link to the earliest days of the national game. Together with his now deceased brother Harry, George Wright had brought professional baseball to Boston more than three decades earlier.

Growing up in New York, Wright played both baseball and cricket. At age fifteen, he became an assistant professional with the St. George Cricket Club and a member of the New York Gothams senior baseball club. Paid under the table to play shortstop for various amateur teams, Wright established a national reputation for his fielding ability and strong arm. In 1904, *Sporting News* recalled Wright's prominence in the early days of the sport:

> Whenever he would pull off one of those grand, unexpected plays that were so dazzlingly surprising as to dumbfound his opponents, his prominent teeth would gleam and glisten in an

array of white molars that would put our own Teddy Roosevelt and his famed dentistry far in the shadow.

The Origins and Development of the National Game

Wright excelled at playing a game that had developed in American cities before the Civil War. In the mid-1840s, young men in cities along the eastern seaboard began playing the game of "base" as an athletic diversion from their white-collar jobs. The game derived from earlier versions of bat-and-ball games that had been played in America since it was settled by Europeans. Even earlier, Native Americans had invented their own stick-and-ball game, now called lacrosse.

In the early nineteenth century, cricket was the most popular sport in America. The British game of rounders, however, became a common alternative for those unwilling or unable to devote the multiple days cricket demanded as a sport. As a letter to *Century Magazine* reported in 1889, boys loved rounders, taking "great delight" in "corking," which was to hurl the ball with as much force as possible at any player who was running between bases. (In its early days, "base ball" or "town ball" also offered a similar method of putting out a player by hitting him with the thrown ball. So-called soaking was abandoned because of the injuries it caused.)

In an article titled "Our National Game" printed in 1871 in *Appleton's Journal,* a weekly publication on literature, science, and art, commentator William R. Hooper extolled baseball's virtues:

Base-ball, restrained within proper limits, is healthy, pleasant, social and uncertain. It has passed from city to town, from town to village, till it has overspread the nation. A thriving town in the West is said to have one church, one school-house, and eight base-ball clubs. It is as much our national game as cricket is that of the English. Both are ball-games played with almost the same number of players. But cricket is slow and unwieldy, more likely to do injury, more scientific in its nature, more

> certain in its result. Base-ball is quick in its evolutions and renew-
> als, gives more opening to dash and energy, depends somewhat
> on luck, and thus gives more chance for betting. . . . Our na-
> tional characteristics develop themselves even in our amuse-
> ments. [Base-ball] is the play of Young America.

A quarter-century earlier on a bluff above Hoboken, New Jersey, in the early summer of 1845, a twenty-five-year-old surveyor and volunteer fire-man, Alexander Cartwright, and the young men who were members of his social club, the New York Knickerbockers, first played the sport we might recognize today as baseball. They had earlier engaged in similar contests on the fields at New York's Madison Square, but as Gotham matured com-mercially that valuable plot of land was developed into a railroad terminal. Undaunted, the participants crossed the Hudson by ferry, each paying the 13¢ fare. They leased a cricket pitch called Elysian Fields for their athletic exercise. On June 19, 1846, Cartwright recorded that they played against a collection of New Yorkers assembled for the occasion on a field laid out as a diamond. The four sides of the diamond were each forty-two paces, almost exactly ninety feet. Each team had three outs to an inning. Both of those innovations distinguished this new game from its predecessors. Cartwright wrote down the rules of the new sport, and within a decade this so-called New York game was played in cities on the East Coast.

A sport for participants and later for spectators, the game of "base" grew in popularity after, and as a result of, the Civil War. Civil War combatants had played baseball during those long periods of tedious waiting between brief interludes of frightening savagery. It is said that President Lincoln favored the game and even intervened on behalf of soldiers ordered to stop playing on the White House lawn. It was played by prisoners of war on both sides. When the soldiers returned home, they spread word of the new pastime nationwide. More streamlined than English cricket, the game of base caught the nation's fancy. (Some, of course, thought all sports an abomination. George Bernard Shaw would later write: "Baseball has the great advantage over cricket of being sooner ended.")

The game of baseball was nurtured in the nation's growing cities, and it would soon assume a pivotal role in American culture. Mark Twain called this game of baseball "the very symbol, the outward and visible expression of the drive and push and rush and struggle of the raging, tearing, booming nineteenth century." In addition to playing the game, a growing number of Americans were willing to pay to watch it played at the highest level of skill. Amateur clubs (sometimes supplemented by paid ringers) played challenge matches against cross-city rivals. The best clubs barnstormed from city to city, taking on all comers.

In the late 1860s, entrepreneurs from Cincinnati asked George Wright's older brother Harry to assemble an all-professional team that would represent the Queen City in challenge matches against clubs around the country. (Actually, there may have been earlier professional clubs, but Wright's team was the first openly professional outfit.) Harry's first choice for the new Red Stockings squad was his brother George, a heavy-hitting shortstop. Wright's Cincinnati Red Stockings toured nationwide in 1869, beating all comers — more than sixty games without a loss — and, in the process, established the supremacy of the professional game over its amateur counterpart. The next season, the Reds won another twenty-four games in a row before losing their first match in an extra-innings contest against the Brooklyn Athletics. Curiously, the traveling Cincinnati Red Stockings never played a home match in Cincinnati.

In 1871, Harry Wright relocated his Red Stockings club to Boston (once again with George Wright at shortstop) as part of the new National Association of Professional Base Ball Players. George Appleton, a local businessman, assisted the Wrights in their effort to bring professional baseball to the Hub. (More than thirty years later, Appleton would attend every Boston game of the 1903 World Series.) Wright's club played at the South End Grounds off Columbus Avenue and adjacent to the New Haven railroad tracks. (The railroad engineers would often stop their locomotives to watch the afternoon games.) The wooden structure had a capacity of six thousand, and, unlike other teams in the new circuit, the club prohibited gambling and the sale of liquor. The Boston entry captured the league pennant each year from 1872 until 1875. During the 1875 season, the club was undefeated at home, amassing thirty-seven victories without a loss or tie. George Wright was the National Association's leading hitter. The club went through changes in leagues and nicknames ("Beaneaters," "Rustlers," and "Braves," to name only a few), a move to Milwaukee in 1953, and another move to Atlanta in 1966. However, the franchise that began in 1871 as Wright's Boston Base Ball Association is the oldest professional ball club to continue without interruption to the present day.

Although the lineage of the original game to the modern sport is direct, the rules of the game in the 1870s differed substantially from those under which the first World Series was played three decades later. As in cricket, pitchers would take a running start before delivering the ball, but unlike cricket, the throw would be underhand. The batter could request a "high pitch" above the waist or a "low pitch" below the waist. Pitches not within the requested zone were considered balls, but it took as many as nine of those offerings before a walk was called. A foul ball caught on the first bounce was an out, and a ball hit fair that then went foul (the so-called fair-foul hit) was in play, even if it crossed the foul line before the base. Players did not generally use gloves until the late 1870s, and when they were introduced, fielders would cut off the fingers of the "mittens" (later shortened to "mitt") to get a better feel of the ball. Harvard's Jim Tyng wore the first catcher's mask in 1877, a device invented by his teammate Fred Thayer to induce Tyng to abandon the outfield for the arduous duties behind the plate. In fairly short order, all catchers adopted the "cage" for protection.

Some commentators, such as a writer in *Nebulae* in 1873, saw baseball as a passing fancy: "[E]ighteen lunatics were racing about, eager to prove the superiority of red stockings over blue or white, and vice versa." Despite these occasional criticisms, the game spread and prospered. Phillip Quilibet, in his *Driftwood* column written in 1871, stated that baseball had won the affection of the multitudes:

> [A]sk for a book-keeper, a mechanic, a tradesman, a down-town friend, the odds are that he has gone to some match between

> the Hittites and Gittites; scarcely a village is without its club, and
> cities have hundreds; fields are alive with athletes; open town
> lots are seized by squatter sovereignty for the game; youngsters
> not yet in their teens throw the ball and strike it with true aim
> and measure of distance, or catch the hot missile with palms
> and wrists of iron. The cant phrase is just—this *is* "the national
> game," and one for us to be quite as nationally proud of as the
> Romans were of their gymnastic ball-game.

Baseball found many devoted adherents in New England. One of the
first college games was held in the Berkshire Hills in Pittsfield, Massachusetts, in 1859 between Amherst and Williams Colleges. Amherst prevailed
73–32. The colleges' avid rivalry continues to this day.

In the winter of 1876 in the back room of a restaurant in downtown
New York City, William Hulbert, a coal operator from Chicago and the owner
of the White Stockings club of that city, joined eight independently owned
franchises together to form the National League. By 1879, the "magnates,"
as the owners called themselves, agreed not to compete for athletes "reserved" by another club. Rival baseball leagues—the American Association
from 1882 until 1891 and the Union Association in 1884—also agreed to
respect the National League's reserve system as long as their own reserved
players were also beyond reach.

George Wright played a total of seven seasons in the National League.
By the mid-1880s, however, Harry and George Wright had turned their
attention to the sporting goods business, Wright & Ditson, that they had
established in Boston. In 1905, Albert Spalding, baseball's most important
business entrepreneur of the nineteenth century, appointed George Wright
to serve on a blue-ribbon commission that would establish "once and for
all" the American origins of the national game. Spalding was convinced that
baseball could not possibly have been of English ancestry. The commission
reviewed flimsy evidence—a single letter from eighty-year old Abner Graves,
who vaguely recalled that Abner Doubleday had established the rules of
the game in Cooperstown, New York, around 1839. (In fact, Doubleday

had never been to Cooperstown in his life, and by 1839 he was a student at West Point.) The commission's final report, issued on December 30, 1907, anointed the deceased Civil War general as the creator of baseball.

Hulbert's National League prospered as the American public found baseball a lively entertainment—and not incidentally a gambling opportunity. The players, however, chafed under the restrictions of the reserve system. In 1885, led by the New York Giants stellar hurler (and Columbia University lawyer) John Montgomery Ward, the players responded to the collusion among the owners by forming the first players' union, the Brotherhood of Professional Base Ball Players. The owners would not address the players' concerns, however. Frustrated in its failed efforts to obtain better terms and conditions of employment, Ward's union created a league of its own in 1890, the Players League, and attracted all the star "ballists" from the established leagues. Spectators at the Players League games—the new circuit outdrew the established leagues—certainly enjoyed its higher level of play. The Boston franchise, the Reds, was led by its popular Irish player-manager, Mike "King" Kelly. Playing at the Congress Street Grounds in South Boston, the club captured the first and only Players League pennant, besting John Ward's New York club by six and a half games. National League business maneuvers—some legal, others not—caused the financial backers of the Players League to fold their rival enterprise after one season. It would be a decade before another circuit would pose a challenge to the established National League.

After the demise of the Players League, baseball prospered without the inconvenience of having to address the concerns of its players. *Sporting News* reported in 1891 that "no game has taken so strong a hold on Americans as base ball." It was the national game, played by young boys on sandlots and by adults after work and on weekends. Reports of professional games filled the new sporting pages of the daily press. Baltimore's James Cardinal Gibbons praised the activity: It was "a healthy sport, and since the people of the country generally demand some sporting event for their amusement, I would single this out as the best to be patronized and heartily approve of it as a popular pastime."

The Creation of the American League

The turn of the twentieth century was a tumultuous time for the national game. After the demise of the American Association in 1891, the National League absorbed four of its abandoned franchises. The quality of play deteriorated during the 1890s, however, and attendance lagged as a result. A single twelve-team major league could not sustain fan interest, especially for those clubs mired in the second division by early summer. New York, Philadelphia, and Chicago, the league's three largest cities, hosted particularly woeful teams. Play on the field and fan behavior off the field had become raucous and ill-tempered, filled with profanity. George Wright, in an interview for *Sporting Life,* an influential weekly tabloid of the time, said: "It is impossible for a respectable woman to go to the games in the National League without running the risk of hearing language which is disgraceful." The *Boston Globe* in 1896 wrote: "Where, oh where, is the National League drifting to?"

In 1898, at the urging of John Brush, then owner of the Cincinnati Reds, the National League adopted the Brush Purification Plan, under which a player using filthy language could be fined, suspended, or banished for life. John McGraw, one of the perennial offenders in this regard, worried that the plan might require him to "abandon my profession entirely." He had no need to worry; the Brush Purification Plan was never enforced.

The magnates were not worried about "purification," but they were concerned about weak franchises. Led by Andrew Freedman, the Tammany-backed owner of the New York Giants, the National League in 1900 jettisoned its four weakest clubs—Cleveland, Louisville, Washington, and Baltimore—paying those owners $104,000 out of the future gate receipts of the remaining clubs. The *New York Times* reported that this move would be "the salvation of the circuit." Instead of salvation, the contraction left four major markets ripe for picking by other enterprising entrepreneurs.

The National League owners remained in disarray, divided over another plan hatched by Freeman to merge the eight remaining clubs into a single trust. Albert Spalding, the league's strongman a decade earlier, came out of retirement to successfully fight the syndicalist maneuver. Adding to this business chaos was the effort by the players to organize a new union to represent their interests. The country had now recovered from the depression of the mid-1890s, and, with general prosperity at hand, it was the opportune moment for the creation of a rival professional baseball league.

Bancroft "Ban" Johnson recognized the time was right for an attack on the National League's monopoly over major league commercial sports entertainment. In 1900, there were no professional football or basketball leagues to compete for the public's entertainment dollar. One-third of Americans lived in major cities. Johnson was the president of a minor league of midwestern clubs, called the Western League. The son of an Ohio college professor, Johnson had attended Marietta and Oberlin Colleges and had played baseball at the collegiate and semiprofessional levels. A sportswriter for the *Cincinnati Commercial-Gazette* from 1887 to 1894, Johnson's involvement with professional baseball would change the game he loved. He had agreed to run the minor Western League to put into effect the changes he thought essential to the game's preservation and success.

Johnson rejected the rowdyism of the play on the field that typified the National League product in the 1890s. With only one umpire on the field for regular season games, players took advantage of every opportunity to bend the rules and even disrupt the play of their opponents. Fielders would trip base runners or hold their belts when they attempted to tag up after a fly out. Base runners, in turn, would take shortcuts home directly from second base if the umpire's attention was elsewhere. Fielders would flash mirrors into the eyes of batters and stash extra balls in the high outfield grass. Fans, or "cranks" as they were commonly called, participated in the onslaught. George Bernard Shaw observed:

> What is both surprising and delightful is that spectators are allowed, and even expected, to join in the vocal part of the game. . . . There is no reason why the field should not try to put the batsman off his stroke at the critical moment by neatly timed disparagements of his wife's fidelity and his mother's respectability.

Baseball in the 1890s was a rough-and-tumble game. Patsy Tebeau, the manager of the Cleveland club, said, "A milk-and-water, goody-goody player can't wear a Cleveland uniform." Umpire Tim Hurst once had eight Cleveland players arrested during a game. (Few umpires would sink to the level of Robert Ferguson, however, who in 1873 reportedly took a bat and broke both arms of the catcher who had complained about Ferguson's calls the entire game. After the game, the authorities arrested Ferguson for assault.)

Johnson would mandate and enforce respect for his umpires, who had often been threatened and even openly attacked during games by players and the "cranks" in the stands unhappy about their decisions. A sign in the ballpark in Kansas City in 1882 read: "PLEASE DO NOT SHOOT THE UMPIRE. HE IS DOING THE BEST HE CAN." Spectators threw beer glasses at opposing players on the field and stoned their horse-drawn coaches on the way to and from the ball field. By the end of the century, Johnson recognized that the deterioration of play on the field and the confusion among the ownership in the National League presented a singular opportunity. He would steer his minor league directly toward major league status and in the process reform the national game.

The successful creation of the American League was the result of fortitude, business skill, and good fortune. Without question, full credit for the venture must go to the thirty-six-year-old driven, overweight moose of a man, Ban Johnson, whose single-mindedness and egotism would not countenance failure. Supported by his lifelong friend, Charles Comiskey, and the seemingly endless financial resources of a young Cleveland merchant and industrialist, Charles A. Somers, who had accumulated a fortune from his coal, lumber, and shipping enterprises, Johnson orchestrated his business plan.

In order to transform a regional minor circuit into a major league, Johnson needed to mold and market an entertainment product that baseball fans in the country's major cities would pay to watch in lieu of the established league. He believed that fans would come out to see a "clean" brand of baseball. *Sporting News* commented that Johnson's Western League thrived because of the absence of "cowardly truckling, alien ownership, . . . selfish jealousies, arrogance of club owners, mercenary spirit, and disregard of public demands." Instead, it had a single-minded autocrat, Ban Johnson.

In October 1899, Johnson changed the name of his circuit to the American League—he thought the name more patriotic—and relocated the St. Paul club to Chicago and the Grand Rapids club to Cleveland. In an October meeting in Chicago after the 1900 season, the new league dropped the Minneapolis, Indianapolis, and Kansas City franchises and moved into Philadelphia, Baltimore, and Washington. Three months later, the American League owners transferred into an escrow account under Johnson's management 51 percent of the stock of each of their clubs and the leases to their stadiums, thus centralizing his control. On January 28, 1901, Johnson transferred the Buffalo franchise to Boston. With these commercial arrangements now embodied in a ten-year agreement, Johnson was ready for a direct confrontation with the Nationals. In February 1901, he made public his challenge:

> The National League has taken it for granted that no one had a right to expand without first getting its permission. We did not think that this was necessary, and have expanded without even asking for permission. . . . If we had waited for the National League to do something for us, we would have remained a minor league forever. The American League will be the principal organization of the country within a very short time. Mark my prediction.

The next critical step would be to attract the stars of the National League to play in Johnson's organization. Success here would ensure ultimate victory.

The new league would also need stadiums to play in, and finding a location in Boston was a particular challenge. Johnson sent Connie Mack, a former star ballplayer and part owner of the new Philadelphia franchise in Johnson's circuit, to Boston to identify property for a new field. In the "Village," an Irish working-class neighborhood west of downtown near Roxbury and adjoining the New Haven Railroad repair yard and roundhouse, Mack sublet a large plot of land from the Boston Elevated Railroad that earlier had been used for circuses, carnivals, and Buffalo Bill's Wild West Show.

The plot of land Mack selected was generally referred to as the Huntington Avenue Carnival Lot. It also had featured a water park called "Shoot the Chutes" with slides and an artificial pond used for skating in the winter. The New England Manufacturers' and Mechanics' Institute erected a huge exhibition hall on the site in the 1880s, advertised as "ten acres of indoor space," the largest structure of its kind in the country.

Boston club owner Charles Somers authorized the construction of a grandstand for the new field on Huntington Avenue, and ground was broken on March 9, 1901. A longtime Boston baseball fanatic named Arthur "Hi Hi" Dixwell (reportedly he would greet all with the phrase "Hi, Hi") was given the honor of turning the first shovel of dirt. Dixwell was known for showering favors on the ballplayers, including frequent gifts of boxes of cigars. *Sporting News* reported: "He lives for the National Game."

The entire construction of the new park was completed for $35,000 and included a locker room for the home nine and "shower baths," a new plumbing innovation. The field, while adequate, was not the finely groomed lawn of today's ballparks. The outfield still had patches of sand from its previous use as a site for circuses. A toolshed stood in fair territory in deep center field.

In January 1901, Johnson drew up a list of the forty-six National League stars who would be enticed to play in the new American League. At the turn of the century, the National League's star players were restless. Their salaries were capped by an immutable individual limit of $2,400 (most were paid less), and they were bound for life by the reserve system to a single club. National League players formed a new alliance in June 1900 to represent their interests. The Players' Protective Association, led by Charles Louis "Chief" Zimmer of the Pittsburgh club and Hughie Jennings of Baltimore, would help the American League's business prospects. A rival league, of course, would provide a competitive purchaser for the players' services and drive up salaries. Former ballplayer Harry Taylor served as the association's attorney and sought modest modifications in the reserve system from the National League magnates, who rejected them out of hand. Ban Johnson, however, on behalf of his American League, quickly adopted the association's proposal for a liberalized uniform player contract. Informally, the union gave its members the go-ahead to seek employment in the new American League.

Using little more than a few extra hundred dollars by way of incentives, together with the blessings of the Players' Protective Association, the American League raiders were wildly successful. They respected existing contracts between players and their National League club owners but ignored the perpetual option clause that was the basis of the National League's restrictive reserve system. All but one of the targeted forty-six players, Pittsburgh's loyal Honus Wagner, would eventually jump to the new circuit.

In March 1901, Johnson's American League made headlines when Charles Somers signed the Boston Beaneaters' Jimmy Collins, the finest third baseman of the day. A few years earlier, Collins had revolutionized play around the "hot corner." Traditionally, the third sacker would field the position standing near the bag, leaving to the shortstop the responsibility for all grounders to his left and ignoring the ever-present threat of a bunt. During a contest between the Louisville Colonels and the Baltimore Orioles in 1895, the Louisville third baseman Walter Preston did just that, allowing the Orioles to successfully bunt seven times down the third-base line. John J. McCloskey, the Louisville manager, offered Fred Clarke — the left fielder who would captain the Pittsburgh club in the 1903 World Series — an extra $50 a month to play third. Clarke declined the invitation, having played the infield without much success earlier in his career. Clarke suggested using rookie outfielder Jimmy Collins. Collins was moved to third. Unfamiliar with the "traditions" of the position, Collins charged in on bunt attempts and threw barehanded to first base. He later recalled that the first batter "bunted and I came in as fast as I dared, picked up the ball, and threw it underhanded to first base. He was out. [Wee Willie] Keeler tried it, and I nailed him by a step. I had to throw out four bunters in a row before the Orioles quit bunting." Soon all third basemen would follow Collins's lead in fielding bunts at third.

At the close of the 1895 season the Boston Beaneaters' purchased

Collins's contract; he became an instant favorite of baseball fanatics in Irish Boston. The "cranks" packed the shabby South End Grounds on Columbus Avenue to cheer for Collins, pitcher Kid Nichols, and outfielders Hugh Duffy and Billy Hamilton as the local club won the National League pennant in 1897 and 1898. In 1901, Collins signed as the player-manager of the new American League entry for $5,500, an astounding salary at the time. (In a few years, he was earning $10,000 a season plus 10 percent of the gate.) As the undisputed leader of the new American League club, Collins convinced three other Beaneater stars—Chick Stahl, Buck Freeman, and Ted Lewis—to join the American side.

Ban Johnson's league continued to score publicity triumphs even before the first game was played. Owner Charles Somers procured a bevy of established players for his Boston club, including the greatest pitcher of the era, Denton True "Cy" Young. Young was not alone in jumping to the fledgling circuit. In fact, of the 185 players on American League club rosters, 111 were former National Leaguers, including some of the senior circuit's greatest stars.

Philadelphia Phillies second baseman Napolean Lajoie, baseball's leading hitter, signed to play for Connie Mack of the cross-town American League rival, the Philadelphia Athletics. The National League owners fought back using the courts, claiming that under the reserve system their players had promised not to play for any other baseball club. Lajoie's case was followed closely in the daily press. When the trial court refused to enjoin Lajoie from playing the 1901 season for the Athletics, the American League had its opportunity to sell its best product to the public. Ultimately, it would be at the turnstiles and not the courthouse that the great baseball war would be won or lost. During its first season, the American League drew 1,658,000 fans, only 200,000 fewer than the National League, even though American League cities had substantially smaller populations than National League cities.

Ban Johnson believed he could replicate on the major league level the "improvements" he had instituted in the Western League. American League baseball would not simply mirror the existing rowdy play on the field that had become the norm. He recalled thirty years later:

> My determination was to pattern baseball in this new league
> along the lines of scholastic contests, to make ability and brains
> and clean, honorable play, not the swinging of clenched fists,
> coarse oaths, riots or assaults upon the umpires, decide the issue.

National League managers and players would "kick" against the decisions of umpires, often baiting the crowd into physically attacking the on-field arbiters. Perhaps the least effective rule in the history of baseball was the 1882 edict that spectators "hissing or hooting at the umpire are to be promptly ejected from the grounds." Normally, only one umpire worked a game, but on occasion two were assigned for mutual protection. Foremost among the offending players was John McGraw of the National League Baltimore Orioles.

Johnson's relationship with John McGraw is one of the more curious stories involved in the start-up of the rival circuit. The twenty-seven-year-old McGraw was enticed by the possibility of owning part of the Baltimore team in the new league, and Johnson appreciated McGraw's drawing power. It was fatuous from the beginning, however, for Johnson to think he could reform the "Little Napoleon."

McGraw's stay in the American League was marked by repeated run-ins with Johnson and multiple league-ordered suspensions. His final suspension, this one for an indefinite period of time, resulted from his refusal to go to the clubhouse after umpire Tommy Connolly ejected him from a game in early July 1902. Midway through the 1902 season, McGraw jumped back to the National League to manage and play for the New York Giants, where he would stay for more than thirty years. McGraw announced to a Baltimore newspaper that it would have been "merely foolishness" to stay with the Americans: "I am harassed and nagged by the umpires until I am put out" of the game. McGraw would hold a lifetime grudge against Johnson, and for Johnson the animosity was mutual.

McGraw's defection almost sunk the new circuit, because the new Giants manager engineered the transfer of the best Orioles players to the New York National League squad. (He even stole the Orioles' groundskeeper,

John Murphy.) Johnson quickly took control of the Baltimore franchise and borrowed players from other clubs to allow the club to finish the season. Following the 1902 season, after reaching a deal with a Tammany Hall faction that opposed Giants owner Andrew Freedman, Johnson moved the Baltimore franchise to New York in direct competition with McGraw's Giants. The Tammany group helped Johnson acquire land at 168th Street and Broadway for a ballpark for the New York Highlanders, as they were to be known. Johnson cleverly covered his ethnic and urban bases when he awarded the valuable New York franchise to poolroom entrepreneur Frank Farrell, who was Jewish, and former New York City police chief William Devery, an Irish-Catholic Tammany insider. He also stocked the club with fine ballplayers, which allowed the new Highlanders to play competitive ball.

By the close of the second year of warfare, it was clear to the National League magnates that Johnson had demonstrated the staying power of his circuit. Even Albert Spalding's *Guide to Baseball* had to admit that "the American League has more star players and can furnish a better article of baseball than the National League." American League attendance in 1902 exceeded National League attendance by more than a half-million patrons. Most of the National League's stars had deserted to the new league. Both National League pennants had been won by Barney Dreyfuss's Pirates, the second by more than twenty-seven games, the widest margin in baseball history. After Honus Wagner had refused to defect, Johnson deliberately left the Pirates club intact for two years and without in-city competition from a rival American League entry, even though the large Pittsburgh market could probably have supported two clubs. As a result of the runaway pennant race and less attractive performers, fans lost interest with the National League product, which helped the American League's cause.

After the 1902 season, Ban Johnson approached Barney Dreyfuss with an offer to bring his entire Pirates squad over to the American League. Dreyfuss declined, and Johnson then proceeded to raid the Pirates' den, signing six regulars to American League contracts. National League magnates were now ready to surrender.

Peace

On December 9, 1902, the National League owners met at the Victoria Hotel in New York to discuss their circumstances. St. Louis owner Frank Robison proposed that a committee be created "for the purpose of conferring with representatives of the American League." Ban Johnson was in New York at the same time meeting with his owners. Johnson and Charles Somers were eating dinner at the Criterion Hotel on the evening of December 11 when they were approached by Frank Robison, James Hart, and August Herrmann (nicknamed "Garibaldi," which was shortened to "Garry") of the National League. Johnson later recalled: "I knew in an instant the purpose of their visit and after greetings all around they informed me [that] they composed a committee of the old league to wait on me and see if peace terms could be arranged." They scheduled peace talks to commence in Cincinnati's St. Nicholas Hotel on January 9, 1903.

In Cincinnati, the representatives of the leagues — Ban Johnson and Charles Comiskey for the American League, Henry Pulliam and Garry Herrmann for the National League — quickly resolved thorny issues of territorial claims and player distribution. They agreed to common playing rules and a minor league draft system. By all reports, it was Herrmann who made sure the peace conference would succeed. As an experienced politician from Cincinnati, Garry Herrmann knew how to make the deal. Under the National Agreement, a National Commission would govern the sport at the major league level. The presidents of the two leagues (Johnson and Pulliam) would serve on the commission that was chaired by a third person selected by the two presidents. They selected Garry Herrmann, the owner of the Cincinnati ball club and a longtime friend of Ban Johnson, thus assuring that Johnson was really in charge. *Sporting Life* puffed that this "ever-memorable joint conference" assured "a brighter and better era for the national sport than it has ever before enjoyed." Both leagues ratified the Cincinnati Peace Agreement on January 19, 1903, and Ban Johnson would run baseball for the next seventeen years, until the creation of the commissioner's office in 1920.

Prior Postseason Challenge Matches

It is curious that the Cincinnati pact did not provide for a postseason contest between the winners of the leagues' pennants. Before the turn of the century, professional baseball leagues had arranged a series of postseason championships to satisfy fans who wanted more baseball and were willing to pay admission to see it. The first contest in 1882 between the Chicago champions of the National League and the Cincinnati club of the American Association ended after they split two games. These were more in the nature of exhibitions than true championship contests. In 1884, however, the Providence Grays of the National League played the American Association's Metropolitan Club of New York "for the championship of the United States," a three-game series in which Providence won every contest, outscoring the Mets 20–3. Attendance for all three games held at New York's Polo Grounds totaled only four thousand. *Sporting Life* proclaimed the victorious Providence nine as the "Champions of the World."

The National League and the American Association played a postseason series each year until 1890, following a variety of formats. In 1885, for example, the series between the American Association's St. Louis club and the National League's Chicago club was played in four different cities. The teams split seven games, winning three apiece with one game called a draw. By 1886, the postseason contests began to draw larger crowds, between six thousand and ten thousand per game. The series was extended to fifteen games in 1887, contracted to ten games in 1888, the best of eleven games in 1889, and the best of five games in 1890. The 1890 series was particularly demoralizing, because that season the nation's best baseball players had deserted the major leagues to play in the outlawed Players League, which was not involved in the postseason event.

The demise of the Players League after its inaugural season and the American Association after the 1891 campaign left the National League as a twelve-club circuit with no rival to challenge postseason. The magnates again tried a variety of postseason formats, but none fully captured the public's attention. In 1892, the regular season was divided in half and the winner of the first half, the Boston Beaneaters, faced off against the winner of the second half, the Cleveland Spiders, in a best-of-nine series won easily by the Boston club, five games to none, with one tie contest called on account of darkness. There was little fan interest in the event because the two clubs had played each other throughout the season, and there was not much uncertainty as to which club would prevail. Two years later, Pittsburgh sportsman William Chase Temple, former owner of the Pirates, donated a silver trophy to go to the winner of a postseason series between the first- and second-place clubs in the league, and well-attended games were held from 1894 until 1897. (William Chase Temple would be in attendance for the Pittsburgh games of the 1903 World Series.) One last best-of-five series in 1900, this time for the Chronicle–Telegraph Cup, ended the "premodern" history of postseason events.

None of these series attracted the attention that the first "modern" postseason series would garner in 1903 (at least in Boston and Pittsburgh) and in the decades to follow as the postseason event became an American tradition. Those earlier contests lacked permanence and stability, always a problem in the early days of professional baseball. There were some spirited games, but none are remembered today.

"The Time Has Come"

The 1903 regular season produced two runaway victors, the mighty Pittsburgh Pirates, who captured their third straight National League title, and the Boston Americans, who had won their first league crown. After the Cincinnati Peace Agreement, Charles Somers sold his Boston club to Milwaukee attorney Henry J. Killilea. Although Killilea was an absentee owner for most of the season, his new club proved profitable and successful on the field.

In early August, Pirates owner Barney Dreyfuss challenged the Boston club to a postseason championship series. Dreyfuss had appreciated the American League's forbearance in not putting a rival team in his city during the war between the leagues. In fact, following the Pirates' pennant win in 1902, Dreyfuss had challenged the American League victor, the Philadelphia

Athletics, to an exhibition series and offered to allow the Athletics to add other American League all-stars to their squad. The four-game event, which was not well publicized, went to the National Leaguers two games to one with one contest ending in a tie.

In 1903, Dreyfuss wrote to Killilea, inviting the challenge match:

> The time has come for the National League and American League to organize a World Series. It is my belief that if our clubs played a series on a best-out-of-nine basis, we would create great interest in baseball, in our leagues, and in our players. I also believe it would be a financial success.

Killilea was new to the organized game. It was his first year (and it would be his last) as a baseball magnate. He had not been part of the American–National war, and thus he did not bear any scars from the economic conflict. Dreyfuss had emerged from the battle virtually unscathed. His humane and generous treatment of his regulars had kept them loyal to the Pirates. (For example, on a road trip to Chicago, Dreyfuss housed his club at a fancy $5-a-night hotel, and, when their game was rained out, he treated the players to a night at the theater.) All other National League teams suffered significant desertions. Dreyfuss knew that the postseason challenge match had great economic potential and would consummate the marriage between the circuits.

Dreyfuss was an old hand at the national game. He had emigrated at age sixteen from Germany to work as an accountant in his cousins' distillery in Paducah, Kentucky. Dreyfuss quickly became a "ballist," as participants in the game were called at the time. He formed his own club in Paducah in 1885. Two years later, when his cousins' business relocated to Louisville, Dreyfuss purchased stock in that city's Colonels of the American Association. His club would later move to the National League when the American Association folded.

Dreyfuss was sometimes called the "Little Colonel." (He was proud to have been designated a "Kentucky Colonel" by the governor of the Commonwealth and did not seem to care that the appellation was widely distributed.) About five feet tall and weighing around one hundred pounds, the mustachioed Dreyfuss spoke with a heavy German accent his entire life. Dreyfuss was a clever businessman, but he was not a saint. He was always a risk taker in the stock market and at the track. Throughout his career in baseball, he wagered on his own team and, during the off-hours, could often be found at a local racecourse.

In 1899, on orders from his doctor to work where there was more fresh air, Dreyfuss quit his accounting position and bought more stock in the Colonels. In February 1899, at age thirty-four, Dreyfuss became president of the Louisville club, replacing his old friend Harry Pulliam who, in a few years, would become president of the National League. When the National League folded the Louisville franchise before the 1900 season, Dreyfuss purchased from locals William Kerr and Phil Auten a significant interest (47.3 percent) in the Pittsburgh club, paying almost $47,000. He brought with him from the defunct Louisville squad fourteen men who would lead the Pirates to success, including Hall of Famers Honus Wagner, Fred Clarke, and Rube Waddell, plus standouts Deacon Phillippe, Chief Zimmer, Claude Ritchey, and Tommy Leach. Dreyfuss would run his beloved Pirates until 1932.

Before responding to Dreyfuss's challenge to a postseason tournament, Killilea, as an obedient American League owner, sought league president Ban Johnson's approval for the event. After Killilea and manager Jimmy Collins assured the league president that the Boston club would prevail, Johnson acceded. Killilea traveled to Pittsburgh to negotiate the details for a best-of-nine postseason series that was to begin in Boston's Huntington Avenue Grounds on Thursday, October 1, 1903, for the first three games. The Series would then move to Pittsburgh's Exposition Park for the next four games, and then back to Boston to complete the Series, assuming that neither team had won the requisite five games. Each club would "furnish and pay the expenses of one umpire." The minimum price of admission was set at 50¢. The owners would split the box office receipts.

Killilea and Dreyfuss had agreed that no player signed after August 31 would be eligible to play, the first time a postseason challenge match had any such restriction. They left to each owner the obligation to work out payments to the players. That proved easy for Dreyfuss, who had his players under contract until October 15. But Killilea's contracts with the Boston players expired September 30, and his players, led by Young and Criger, threatened not to play the Series unless they received all of Boston's share of the proceeds. The *Pittsburgh Dispatch* attributed the players' "strike" to the fact that Killilea was a "foreign" owner who spent the season in Milwaukee and did not know his Boston charges: "Home capital makes baseball a success." (By comparison, the relationship between President Dreyfuss and his Pittsburgh players was characterized as based on "the best of good feelings.") With some difficulty, Killilea finally reached an arrangement with his players, splitting Boston's share between the owner and the athletes.

The Pirates' triumph in the first game of the World Series had unsettled Boston's fanatics, accustomed to their locals' spirited and successful play. Boston baseball had enjoyed a long history of triumph on the field, starting with the Wright brothers' Red Stockings of the 1870s. A Boston club had been a charter member of the National League and had secured league pennants in 1878, 1883, 1891, 1892, 1893, 1897, and 1898. Boston fandom had quickly switched its allegiance to the new American League entry, making it their own. This long World Series would test their devotion.

The Second Game

On October 3, 1903, the *Boston Herald* reported that

> When Boston went home after the [first] game on Thursday, her brow was knit, her jaw was set; behind her lay the memory of idols overthrown; before her lay the uncertainty of the future, so hazy that it was impossible to predict either darkness or day, and it was with sad misgivings that she laid her head on the pillow that night. And when she rose . . . it was with a keen realization that she must rally her forces. The invading Pirates

must be repulsed at all hazards, and Boston had learned by sad
experience that such a task was work for champions.

Attendance was down on an overcast Friday for the second contest
between Pittsburgh and Boston. Rain threatened and a few sprinkles fell
before the game began. The Friday crowd was decidedly smaller than
Thursday's crush of humanity. There were 9,415 in attendance at the Huntington Avenue Grounds. Nonetheless, this was a record crowd for a Friday
afternoon, and twenty minutes before the game began every seat in the
grandstand was taken.

It was a dreary day for a baseball game. The steady rain after 2:00 P.M.
raised umbrellas, "only to be lowered hastily when the unprotected would
not stand for having their view obstructed." Captain Jimmy Collins answered a question from the crowd as to whether the game would be played
under such conditions: "It will take more than a mist like this to make your
rain check good," responded Boston's cherished third baseman. When the
fog settled in from the northeast, the odds seemed stacked against Collins's
prediction. Yet at 3:00, the gong for play sounded right on schedule, and
umpire Hank O'Day took his place behind the plate.

Despite the inclement weather, the spectators witnessed a masterful
pitching performance by William Patrick "Big Bill" Dineen, whose "good
right arm," the *Boston Post* wrote, "carried the . . . team to a splendid victory." The Americans were determined to "atone for the galling defeat" of
the prior day. Newspapers reported that by game time the betting line for
the second contest again favored a Boston victory. "Sports" needed to place
$1,000 against $800 for the Pittsburgh pikers, although President Dreyfuss
placed a $500 bet on his club at even money.

The Americans showed confidence at bat from the first, scoring two
runs their initial time at bat. Boston's "modest" Pat Dougherty led off with
an inside-the-park home run to deep right-center. (The prior day, that hit
would have been lost in the overflow crowd and would have been a ground-
rule triple.) Dougherty slid home headfirst, beating the relayed throw.
Stahl doubled to center and scored on Freeman's single. The Boston fans

"were in on every play," using horns, whistles, clappers, and voices to cheer on their local favorites. The spectators "cheered themselves hoarse." "Reason, for the moment, gave way to the delirium of joy," but the thirty-five policemen in attendance kept the good-spirited crowd in check: "No trouble of any kind occurred."

Dineen, "cool as an iceberg," faced only twenty-nine batters that afternoon and allowed only three hits as he shut out the Pirates 3–0. On the other hand, Pittsburgh's "Goshen Schoolmaster," Sam Leever, was not at his best. Leever was hit so hard that he left the game after one inning, relieved by the Pirates' diminutive rookie Bucky Veil. The Americans' other tally came in the sixth inning when Dougherty, who accounted for two-thirds of Boston's run production that day, blasted his second home run over the left field wall into Huntington Avenue traffic, only the second time that feat had been achieved in the short history of the ballpark. Jimmy Collins later told reporters that Dougherty's opposite-field stroke was "the greatest hit I ever saw by a left-handed batter." The fans "danced and they shrieked and it was minutes until they came down to earth again."

Newspapers commented on the fine infield play by both clubs, a challenge on the bumpy infield at the Grounds. The *Boston Herald* spouted: "There is no doubt the work of both infields was superior to anything any other two major league teams can show. Both pitchers can thank their elegant support for their effectiveness." By comparison to game one, the Boston outfielders did not have much work to do on a day when Dineen had fine stuff on his pitches.

Dineen held the Pirates' Leach, Wagner, and Bransfield hitless. (They had accumulated six hits in Pittsburgh's victory in game one.) Sebring, who had knocked in four runs the prior day, was held to one two-out fifth-inning single and was left stranded on first base. In a game that took less than two hours to compete, Dineen struck out eleven Pirates.

GAME 2

Team	1	2	3	4	5	6	7	8	9	R	H	E
Pittsburgh	0	0	0	0	0	0	0	0	0	0	3	2
Boston	2	0	0	0	0	1	0	0	x	3	9	0

The *Boston Herald* regaled the local victors as having "torpedoed" the Pirates ship, and the Boston bettors recouped some of their losses from the prior day. "Boston baseballdom smiles once more." The Series was tied at one game apiece. The press predicted that the next day's game would produce "the greatest aggregation" of fans that ever saw a sports contest in Boston, and their prediction was right on the money.

JOHN I. TAYLOR

*"John I.," as he was known, the Brahmin son of the owner
of the* Boston Globe, *had tried the newspaper business but
showed little interest or talent. Baseball was the main focus of
his attention, and he attended every Boston Americans game.
His father despaired at the prospects for his son. Baseball,
it seemed, was John I.'s only interest. In early 1904, General
Charles Taylor bought the Boston franchise for his son.*

3

Boston Proper: The Brahmins and the Yankees

The Huntington Avenue battle between the Pittsburgh nine and the hometown favorites shared the front pages of the local dailies with news of the arrival from London of the British Honourable Artillery Company. The oldest regiment in the British army, it was established under Royal Charter by King Henry VIII in 1537. The British Honourables held the unique privilege of being able to march through the City of London with "drums beating, colours flying and bayonets fixed." The company's assignment was not simply pageantry. It had recently received battle honors for its service in the South African Boer War between 1900 and 1902. America's Anglophiles had prepared elaborate programs for the Honourables' fortnight tour of the former British colonies that would begin and end in Boston. One duke traveling with the entourage opined: "Such visits can only do good and promote harmony between our two great Anglo–Saxon races."

Many Bostonians had little in common with the uniformed guests from London. But for Boston's Brahmin upper class, the Honourables' visit to New England symbolized the historical preeminence of Americans with British ancestry. At the same time that Boston's stalwart baseball nine persevered on the Huntington Avenue diamond, its Anglo plurality reveled in the blue-blooded grandeur of the Honourables' visit. Although members of Boston's elite attended the World Series—and one would purchase the club the following winter—most of their attention was focused on the splendid parties planned for the British visitors. Interestingly, the Boston hosts thought it was important for their British visitors to attend the third game of the World Series.

The City on the Hill

The teeming metropolis of Boston at the turn of the twentieth century was a far cry from the village that first occupied the Shawmut Peninsula almost three hundred years earlier. In 1630, Boston covered 783 acres on a fist of land jutting out into Massachusetts Bay and the huge estuary of the Charles River. Boston's population expanded with new immigrants from the British Isles, and until 1760—when Philadelphia surpassed it—Boston was the largest city in the American colonies.

As a result of landfill projects that started early in the nineteenth century, Boston more than doubled its acreage. Public and private enterprise created land for growth by filling in wharves and bays on all sides of the town. The largest single public-private partnership effort, between the Boston Water Power Company and the State of Massachusetts, filled in more than seven hundred acres of the Back Bay of the Charles River. Dozens of railroad trains carried landfill from the suburban Needham gravel pit west of Boston, nine miles away. The project began in 1857 and took more than thirty years to complete. Developers built fashionable town houses on speculation in the new midcity neighborhood, each brownstone with its own architectural style but within strict zoning requirements enforced by the City of Boston. The homes quickly sold to families seeking more space than crowded properties on Beacon Hill could provide.

By the 1880s, the new Back Bay had become the center of Boston's social and cultural life. Reflecting the Anglo origins of most of its residents, the cross streets of the neighborhood were christened with British names—Arlington, Berkeley, Clarendon, Dartmouth, Exeter, Fairfield, Gainsborough, and Hereford. Laid out like a continental boulevard with a park dividing two roadways, the majestic Commonwealth Avenue connected Massachusetts Avenue with the Public Garden, adorned by a pond and its popular swan boats. South of Boylston Street and west of the downtown of colonial times, on the newly filled-in land between Dartmouth and Clarendon Streets, there arose a new town center called Copley Square, named for Boston-born John Singleton Copley, the first great American painter. Copley's memorable portrait of Paul Revere shows the artisan-turned-radical with an exquisite silver teapot of his making. Despite Copley's great success, he and his Tory wife departed for London in 1774, claiming that his fellow Bostonians were "entirely destitute of all just ideas of the arts."

The cornerstone of Copley Square was the majestic Trinity Church, designed by the young Henry Hobson Richardson in 1872. Although his offices were in New York City, Richardson had strong Boston ties. While an undergraduate at Harvard, he was a member of the Brahmin Procellian Club. (Five of the eleven members of the committee that selected the architect for the new edifice were also alumni of that elite coterie.) A new home for the Episcopal ministry that dated from 1733, Trinity Church was consecrated on February 9, 1877, the first building to occupy Copley Square. It was universally acclaimed (then and now) as one of the nation's finest structures.

On the opposite end of Copley Square stood the Boston Public Library, the nation's first public library. Architect Charles Follen McKim (who had worked in H. H. Richardson's office as a young draftsman) completed his "palace for the people" in 1895. The inscription on its north face summarized the progressive philosophy of the times: "THE COMMONWEALTH REQUIRES THE EDUCATION OF THE PEOPLE AS THE SAFEGUARD OF ORDER AND LIBERTY."

On the south side of Copley Square stood the Museum of Fine Arts, built in the Victorian Gothic style. When in 1907 the museum relocated west on Huntington Avenue just past the Huntington Avenue Grounds, the Copley Plaza Hotel, designed by the distinguished New York architect Henry Janeway Hardenbergh, ably filled the valuable site.

The Boston Brahmin Class

For "the Brahmin caste," Oliver Wendell Holmes wrote, Boston was the "hub of the Universe . . . that blessed centre of New England life." The origin of the name Brahmin as applied to upper-class Bostonians is unclear. One unlikely suggestion is that it originated with the American premiere of Brahms's Second Symphony performed by the Boston Symphony Orchestra at the Orpheum Theatre on Hamilton Place near Tremont Street. Many in the audience walked out of the performance, and music reviewers referred to the stalwarts who stayed as "Brahmins," presumably because of their fondness for Brahms. More likely, patrician Bostonians borrowed the term from that used to describe the highest caste in India, those who by legend were created from the mouth of Brahma to instruct mankind.

Proper Bostonians saw themselves as a "chosen people," fiduciaries for the American enlightenment in the arts, literature, and morality. The Brahmins' cousins, the Yankees, shared their British lineage but had remained farmers, fishermen, and artisans, leaving social, public, and intellectual responsibilities to their wealthy and educated relatives.

By the turn of the twentieth century, however, the "Anglo-Saxon race" had lost its exclusive hold on Boston's commerce and politics. Members of Anglo families who made up "Boston Proper" had been dislodged from their perch by the children and grandchildren of waves of immigrants—first by the Irish in the 1840s and 1850s, and more recently by the southern Italians and eastern Europeans. Of course, the Brahmins and bankers remained the main source of New England's capital and investment, but the immigrants had gained a foothold in the growing mercantile sector.

Disillusioned by the changes in their city and alienated from the masses of non-English-speaking immigrants, the Brahmin natives of Boston were anxious about the future of their commonwealth. They eagerly awaited the visit of the British Honourable Artillery Company, with which they claimed a common bond and heritage. The Honourables' visit would reassure the Brahmins of their proper prominence—if only for a few weeks. If it was fantasy and self-deception, at least it would be a glorious party.

The New England aristocracy was of relatively recent vintage. Although some Anglo families could trace their lineage for eight generations back to the earliest days of settlement of the colony, the Brahmin way of life was the product of only a few decades of mercantile prosperity and higher education. Presidents John Adams and John Quincy Adams, progenitors of a line of Brahmins, were born of humble circumstances on modest farms in Braintree, Massachusetts. Both rose to political heights, but neither would claim that his status was predestined. Their progeny, however, including the paradigm Brahmin, John Quincy's grandson Henry Adams, shouldered their social and moral responsibility as a matter of preordained obligation. Henry Adams, who called himself "the quintessence of Boston," was ultimately disillusioned by this role. His autobiography, *The Education of Henry Adams,* written in the third person, aptly chronicled the decline of the Brahmin fraternity.

Throughout much of the nineteenth century, almost any Yankee male youngster, even one of relatively modest family resources, could aspire to ascend into Brahmin society. According to Samuel Eliot Morison, a Proper Bostonian himself, new families would be accepted into the Brahmin caste as long as they earned enough to purchase a town house on Commonwealth Avenue and a summer place on the North Shore, and educated their children at private schools in the Back Bay.

The metamorphosis from Yankee to Brahmin began at the gates of Harvard College, across the Charles River from Boston. Harvard was common ground for Boston's elite, the intellectual Mecca toward which all Brahmins would turn for guidance and training as well as reassurance of their status. This seat of parochial instruction spawned generations of Proper Bostonians and imbued them with a sense of prerogative balanced with a moral responsibility to protect the inheritance of the Puritans. Controlled by the Unitarian clergy, Harvard College in the nineteenth century transmitted the intellectual products of this heritage to new generations of New England's scions.

Harvard offered its young men a classical education infused with a Unitarian liberal respect for individuality. All male members of the great

Brahmin families attended the Cambridge institution—the Cabots, Lowells, Lodges, Quincys, Phillipses, Shattucks, Holmeses, Eliots, Peabodys, and Adamses. These young graduates of Harvard would be charged with the obligations of stewardship that required courageous decision making. By comparison, a mere pedestrian New Englander, according to Henry Adams, demonstrated

> the habit of doubt; of distrusting his own judgment and of totally rejecting the judgment of the world; the tendency to regard every question as open; the hesitation to act except as a choice of evils; the shirking of responsibility [and] the horror of ennui.

In Harvard lectures, Brahmin ideals of individuality, first espoused in the eighteenth century by the nation's founders, were embellished with "modern" Teutonic theory. It was essentially a race-based dogma but imbued with religious tolerance, respect for the individual, and faith in the perfectibility of man. With a self-assumed moral superiority came the concomitant obligation to safeguard the destiny of the city of the Brahmins as well as the region and the nation. Harvard's James Russell Lowell warned against the "dead level of commonplace," and his disciples carried forth the charge.

The cultivation of the Brahmin class did not prepare these chosen few to face the rapidly changing social and economic landscape of Boston. The city's economic base had been built on trade. The grand clipper ships had plied the seas from Boston, and the merchant class accumulated wealth. Boston banks supplied the capital for these ventures, which often included profits from the slave trade. By midcentury, however, the factory system of manufacturing in Massachusetts towns such as Lowell, Lawrence, and Haverhill had triumphed. The economy evolved from one based on agriculture and handiwork to what Henry Adams called "the great mechanical energies—coal, iron, steam."

The Brahmins found Boston's new immigrant inhabitants rather peculiar but, at least initially, useful additions to the population mix. The Irish and the French Canadians would supply the manual labor needed to support the Hub's economy. At first, many thought the immigrants would easily "combine" with the "native" population—that is, anyone who had immigrated generations earlier—and form a strong amalgam under Brahmin dominance and leadership. They would have to learn how to function in Brahmin-led Boston.

Before the Civil War, Brahmins had strongly opposed the nativist movement that would have limited or eliminated immigration. They had led the national antislavery effort and gloried in the bloody victory over the Southern planter classes that abolished America's peculiar institution. Although Brahmins had found slavery intolerable, they did not believe in racial equality. At the core of Brahmin philosophy was a profound belief in the righteousness of the established caste system.

Although Boston's factories enjoyed a world market for shoes and textiles, its economy did not adapt to the growing continental system of trade with the American West. While New York prospered from its canal and railroad systems, Boston stood isolated on the coast. Boston businesses did not forge the same connections to the future engines of growth. The reliance on old ways in the new economic world inhibited Boston's prosperity and the economic mobility of new classes of potential entrepreneurs.

By the 1880s, Brahmin intellectuals sensed that America and their place in it had changed. The immigrants had decidedly resisted assimilation under Brahmin rule. Instead, they forged a group cohesiveness that would not yield to Brahmin influence, that did not revere the Brahmin point of view or recognize its leadership role in society. Irish immigrants clung closely to their Catholic, conservative way of life while mobilizing a potent political force that challenged and then bested the Brahmins at the polls. The new immigrant underclass brought visions—and at times the reality —of vice, crime, and disease.

As the century closed, Brahmins, with palpable sadness, acknowledged that their society was irreparably bisected into natives and immigrants. Henry Adams wrote, "We had better do our epitaphs and do them quick." Despondent, bewildered, and disturbed by the economic and political advancement of the immigrants, the Brahmins clung to their one remaining advantage: their social distinction.

Brahmins viewed with abhorrence and disgust the immigrants' living conditions. Civil War general Francis A. Walker, a leading Brahmin social scientist and one of the first presidents of the Massachusetts Institute of Technology, described the immigrants' living conditions:

> [Their] houses . . . were mere shells for human habitations, the gate unhung, the shutters flapping or falling, free pools in the yard, and young children rolling half naked or worse, neglected, dirty unkempt.

His disdain for the immigrants was evident in all his writings. His article in the *Atlantic Monthly* of June 1896 explained:

> For nearly two generations, great numbers of persons utterly unable to earn their living, by reason of one or another form of physical or mental disability, and others who were, from widely different causes, unfit to be members of any decent community, were admitted to our ports without challenge or question. . . . That man must be a sentimentalist and an optimist beyond all bounds of reason who believes that we can take such a load upon the national stomach without a failure of assimilation, and without great danger to the health and life of the nation. For one, I believe it is time that we should take a rest, and give our social, political, and industrial system some chance to recuperate. The problems which so sternly confront us to-day are serious enough without being complicated and aggravated by the addition of some millions of Hungarians, Bohemians, Poles, south Italians, and Russian Jews.

Toward the end of the nineteenth century, Brahmin intellectuals and members of the Harvard faculty, heavily influenced by Teutonic racist theory and the reality of nonassimilation, had reversed their position on immigration, which they now strenuously opposed. By the late 1870s, the Irish had developed a political consciousness and taken control of Boston's public services. Harvard College, Henry Adams wrote, was "poor in votes, but rich in social influence." Social influence, however, could not control the ballot box.

In the century's final decade, the second major wave of immigrants descended on Boston, this time from southern and eastern Europe. The Brahmin attitude toward these newcomers turned from alienation to disgust. They saw the continued influx of the canaille from Europe as a catastrophe and argued that the social consequences of continued immigration on the fabric of America were dreadful. American values were jeopardized by the "alien masses" of inferior stock. It was now hopeless to think that absorption and assimilation were possible. With the creation and growth of the Immigration Restriction League, whose mission it was "to save the nation from foreign infiltration," Boston's influentials sought to close the open door through legislation. It would take decades to achieve that goal; by the time new immigration laws were passed, Boston and the nation had changed forever. Finally, the Brahmins retreated from involvement with the "unwashed" public, while they maintained control over their private society and the professions. They celebrated those occasions when the "old stock" could flaunt its historical importance and preeminence, such as the 1903 visit of the British Honourables.

Henry Cabot Lodge and His Fellow Brahmins

Henry Cabot Lodge, the Brahmin senator from Massachusetts, devoted much of his political career to the "immigrant problem." The son of a rich China trade merchant, Lodge graduated from Harvard in 1872, writing his thesis on Anglo-Saxon racial purity. Elected first to the Massachusetts legislature in 1879, then to Congress in 1886, Lodge rose to national prominence in the Senate starting in 1893. Ever vigilant in protecting Massachusetts manufacturing industries from foreign competition, Lodge argued that the native wage earner also needed protection against the immigrant laborers who would work for lower wages. Moreover, Lodge believed that

immigrants from autocratic nations were incapable of meeting the obligations of self-government.

Aided by the Boston-based Immigration Restriction League, which had
a large following in East Coast cities, Lodge pressed his congressional col-
leagues to impose a literacy requirement on immigrants, knowing it would
severely restrict their entrance. In a celebrated speech on the floor of the
Senate on March 16, 1896, Lodge spelled out the danger of free immigration. Immigrants were "strangers" who caused "ethnic deterioration." They
were, Lodge said, "an inferior race." With open immigrant admission to
the country, the descendants of the pure Americans "were doomed." The
survival of the race and the "protection of the blood" were at stake. Lodge's
immigration bill passed Congress in 1896 but was vetoed by President
Cleveland. Congress would not restrict European immigration until the
1921 Johnson Act set ethnic quotas.

Although he may not have attended any baseball contests, Lodge once
had a physical confrontation with a minor league baseball player who
was one of his constituents. On April 2, 1917, Alexander Bannwart visited
Lodge's Senate office to protest his support of President Wilson's request
for a declaration of war. Angry words were exchanged ("liar," "coward"),
followed by shoving. Finally, the sixty-seven-year-old senator punched the
thirty-six-year-old ballplayer in the mouth. Capitol police arrested the ballplayer.

Not all Brahmins shared Lodge's racist views about restricting immigration. Charles W. Eliot, Harvard College president from 1869 to 1909,
steadfastly adhered to policies of free immigration espoused by his predecessors. America could still produce "good families," Eliot reasoned,
while remaining a "civilization in the making." He wrote in 1895:

> The United States have made to civilization a . . . contribu-
> tion of a very hopeful sort, to which public attention needs to
> be directed, lest temporary evils connected therewith should
> prevent the continuation of this beneficent action. The United

> States have furnished a demonstration that people belonging
> to a great variety of races or nations are, under favorable cir-
> cumstances, fit for political freedom. . . . In two respects the
> absorption of large numbers of immigrants from many nations
> into the American commonwealth has been of great service to
> mankind. In the first place, it has demonstrated that people
> who at home have been subject to every sort of aristocratic or
> despotic or military oppression become within less than a gen-
> eration serviceable citizens of a republic; and, in the second
> place, the United States have thus educated to freedom many
> millions of men.

As a matter of Christian charity, some Brahmin women sought to ease the transition for the new arrivals even as their husbands despaired. From their pulpits, clergy called for help for the underprivileged and applauded philanthropy in aid of the immigrants. In settlement houses, such as the South End House, immigrants were offered clothing and food; they were also taught English and job skills to relieve the pressures of urban life. Physical exercise and recreation — the "gospel of play" — was considered essential in promoting public health. Many immigrants learned to play the American game of baseball at these settlement houses. Generous humani-tarianism, however, was the exception rather than the rule.

Despite the presence of immigrants in their town who, for the most part, stayed segregated in their ethnic enclaves, the Brahmins enjoyed the extravagance of life in Boston at the turn of the new century. For the very wealthy, whom Mark DeWolfe Howe called the "cultured, moral and conservative" members of "Boston Proper," it was a time of excess. They enjoyed the arts that Boston could offer — the opera, symphony, and mu-seums that were the epitome of the highest level of American culture of the time. The nation's oldest continuously active performing arts organiza-tion, the Handel and Haydn Society, formed in 1815 by Gottlieb Graupner (who had played under Haydn in London in the late eighteenth century) and a group of Boston merchants, presented regular recitals that were well attended. The organization had offered the American premiere of Handel's *Messiah* in 1818 and Haydn's *The Creation* in 1819, and it was considered by the Brahmins one of the treasures of Boston.

As a boy, Boston philanthropist Henry Lee Higginson went to the opera in London and concerts in Munich, Dresden, and Milan. Thus began an affection for music that would be his lifetime preoccupation. After inheriting a fortune from his uncle and serving in the Civil War, Higginson abandoned his work as a banker to pursue his dream of establishing America's first symphony orchestra, an ensemble that would meet Continental standards. In 1881, he founded the Boston Symphony Orchestra, the pride of all Brahmins. He hired the conductors, paid the musicians, and eventually in 1900 built the acoustically magnificent Symphony Hall on the corner of Massachusetts and Huntington Avenues (within sight of the Huntington Avenue Grounds) using New York's McKim, Mead & White to design the edifice. The acoustics, engineered by the Harvard physicist Wallace Clement Sabine, were remarkable. Symphony Hall remains among the finest concert halls in the world. (Sabine's work in acoustics was truly groundbreaking. In fact, the unit of sound absorption was named the "metric sabin" in his honor.)

Mrs. Isabella Stewart Gardner attended the first open rehearsal of the Boston Symphony in its new Massachusetts Avenue home. She had married a wealthy Boston Brahmin financier, John Lowell Gardner, in 1860 at the age of twenty. (Her own fortune came from her father's department store in New York.) Mr. Gardner was referred to by all as "Jack," and Mrs. Gardner became known as "Mrs. Jack."

Upon her attendance at the rehearsal, the *Boston Journal* remarked that Mrs. Gardner "looked remarkably well in a black crepon gown made with three-fourth-length coat, the waist of which was held in place by a wide jetted belt." In years to come, her influence on the arts in Boston would transcend her wardrobe. Her mansion, Fenway Court, was in the Fens, one block from Huntington Avenue and three blocks from the Huntington Avenue Grounds. She had designed the edifice in the style of a fifteenth-century Venetian palace and opened her home to the public in 1903 as a museum. With galleries built around an interior courtyard filled year-round with blooming flowers, the Isabella Stewart Gardner Museum's paintings, sculpture, and decorative arts remain to this day one of the premier collections in the country.

Four years after the 1903 World Series, Boston's Brahmins would celebrate the groundbreaking of a magnificent new facility for the Museum of Fine Arts, one block from the ballpark on the north side of Huntington Avenue. Directly across Huntington Avenue from the grounds, the new Boston Opera House hosted its premier performance on November 8, 1908. The *Boston Globe* reported that this new home for the opera was the "best equipped temple of music in America." Bounded by Symphony Hall to the east and the Isabella Stewart Gardner Museum to the west, Huntington Avenue had become the center of Boston arts. Almost exactly in the middle of this boulevard stood the local temple of American League baseball.

While the elite favored their high culture, Boston's theaters offered a variety of fare to anyone able to pay the ticket prices. Comedy and light musical entertainment predominated. In 1903, at the new Colonial Theatre on Tremont Street, for example, Jerome Sykes starred in the musical farce *The Billionaire* with the original cast (and a chorus of one hundred) direct from Daly's Theatre in New York City. Ticket prices started at 50¢, and the top ticket was $1.50. At the Mechanics Building across Massachusetts Avenue from Symphony Hall, the Great Fair featured Creatore and his renowned band, a Japanese theater and tea garden with geisha girls, other Asian delights, and a demonstration of Marconi telegraphy. Admission was only two bits.

The Brahmins at Home

In addition to these public diversions of high culture, Brahmins on Beacon Hill and in the Back Bay would entertain members of the elite class in their homes. As Cleveland Amory noted in *The Proper Bostonians:* "Boston debutantes soon learn they must know how to discuss politics, sports and other masculine subjects, or else be still." When hostesses became bored with their own conversation, they hired professional entertainers, singers, clairvoyants, and raconteurs to entertain their guests. After a dinner of eight courses, the women would "retire" to allow their men to smoke, drink, and converse separated from the opposite sex.

Brahmin homes offered the latest conveniences of the day—piped water, electric lighting, furnace heat, water closets connected to the city sewer, and telephones. A bevy of housemaids, cooks, laundresses, and liveried coachmen would provide exquisite service. (Interestingly, Brahmin gentlemen did not favor the British custom of employing valets.)

Upper-class Bostonians dressed their part in elegant frock coats and high hats for men, lace shawls, billowing dresses, and parasols for women. High fashion was "the insignia of leisure," Thorstein Veblen wrote in *The Theory of the Leisure Class.* "Much of the charm that invests the patent-leather shoe, the stainless linen, the lustrous cylindrical hat, and the walking stick . . . comes of their pointedly suggesting that the wearer cannot when so attired bear a hand in any employment that is directly and immediately of any human use."

In addition to their city homes, the upper class would have "cottages" in the country, perhaps in Manchester-by-the-Sea on the North Shore or in Walpole or Canton in the countryside west of the Hub. By the 1890s, members of the upper class were beginning to move their primary residences to the new fashionable suburb of Brookline, said to be the wealthiest town in the world. A decade later, buying summer property in Maine would be all the rage.

Brahmins enjoyed their mobility, social power, and distinction. They took first-class railroad cars to Newport or New Hampshire on holidays. Families sought to cement their ties to Europe through annual pilgrimages. Anglophilia was rampant, but visits to the other countries on the European continent were also obligatory as long as the Brahmins were accompanied by an assortment of maids and nannies.

Brahmins and Baseball

Some Brahmins found their way to the Huntington Avenue Grounds to partake of the national pastime, and their presence was always duly noted by the local press. However, this form of sports entertainment generally was not considered suitable for the upper class. As William R. Hooper wrote in 1871:

> Base-ball is not the game of cultured society. . . . It is gregarious in nature and delights in crowds. The ringing cheer that marks a good catch, the groan that follows the muffin play, the hearty sympathy of the multitude are essential elements in its composition.

It was certainly not a place for women of culture: "Base-ball would seem so far out of line of feminine pursuits that nothing need be said of it," opined Reverend J. T. Crane in the *Ladies' Repository*. But Crane did acknowledge that the sport had become the "national game" to which ladies were invited:

> The game itself is not objectionable. It may be made a very innocent, pleasant, healthful amusement. . . . But . . . it has become a ponderous and elaborate affair. . . . The overwrought excitement, the excessive exertion, absence of mental ease and conversational freedom, condemn it. The publicity of the performance is itself sufficient to nullify all good results. . . . It seems to me that the modern bubble has been blown up so big that it must burst before long.

Although benign in his views about immigration, Harvard president Charles Eliot expressed serious reservations about the sport of baseball. His Crimson nine was one of the nation's premier clubs and, at least in earlier days, had played on a par with professional clubs. Curiously, in the 1870s, Eliot expressed his particular concerns about the curveball. He characterized the pitch as a "low form of cunning." Eliot wrote:

> I heard that this year we won the championship because we have a pitcher who has a fine curve ball. I am further instructed

> that the purpose of the curve ball is to deliberately deceive the batter. Harvard is not in the business of teaching deception.

Eliot also expressed reservations about the pitcher's practice of picking runners off base, considering it "ungentlemanly." He allowed the sport to continue on campus but never became a fan of the game. In an address in 1884, Eliot said:

> I think it is a wretched game, [and] as an object of ambition for the youths to go to college, really it is a little weak. There are only nine men who can play the game, and there are 950 students in Harvard, and out of the nine there are but two desirable positions, I understand — pitcher and catcher — so there is little chance for the youth to gratify his ambition. I call it one of the worst games, although I know it is called the national game of the United States.

Those who did not follow baseball certainly knew of its existence and appreciated its commercial potential. Some upper-class money found its way to the ball field, both as gambling stakes and as business investments. It was, of course, a staple sport of the lads at Harvard, although second in their hearts to the rough-and-tumble of football.

Henry Adams

Although Henry Adams had joined his fellow Brahmins in their distaste for the Irish, by the turn of the twentieth century he had reluctantly accepted the status of the midcentury immigrants. Adams saved his particular disdain for the Jews. "The Hebrews," he wrote in his autobiography, "were pervasive and irrepressible." To Adams, "Jewish" meant greedy, avaricious, and materialistic. The ancient Jews of the Bible were distinguished in his mind from the repugnant modern Jews. Their arrival in Boston made it clear to Adams that the city could never be homogeneous again. At least the Irish had remained apart, educating their young in Catholic schools. The Jews pushed their way into commercial society and, unless resisted, would topple American values and standards in their wake.

Adams had been confident at first that the eighteenth-century "fabric of . . . moral principles" would be preserved despite the immigrants. "Boston had solved the universe," he exclaimed. He believed that "what had been would continue to be," as long as people acted with appropriate restraint and respect for their proper roles in society. He summed up his personal philosophy: "Whether life was an honest game of chance, or whether the cards were marked and forced, he could not refuse to play his excellent hand." Adams was certain he had an excellent hand, but the "game" had changed.

To Adams, the privileged had been "designated by destiny" to find a solution to every problem, but to do so with "balance, judgment [and] restraint . . . free from vanity," Brahmin gentlemen demonstrated the necessary "objectiveness," selflessness of purpose, and "honest courage." Regretfully, "subdivisions of society existed," and the Brahmin class was "thin" and showed "little . . . cohesion." He despaired of Boston's future: "Nowhere in America was society so complex or change so rapid. New power was disintegrating society, and setting independent centres of force to work." The new immigrants played by different, and less diffident, rules. Adams reached for a baseball metaphor to express his angst: "Naturally such an attitude annoyed the players in the game [of politics, society, etc.] as the attitude of the umpire is apt to infuriate the spectators."

There was one last reserve of influence, however. A Brahmin was "English to the last fibre of his thought—saturated with English literature, English tradition, English taste." Adams confessed that "like all Bostonians" he was "instinctively English." If the Brahmins could not maintain their hereditary status and dominance in isolation, they would look to their British kinsmen for inspiration and solace. Anglophilism was pervasive—afternoon tea (both party tea and small tea), the cotillion ball, and fox hunts all reinforced the Brahmins' view of the world. "The true Bostonian," according to Adams, "always knelt in self-abasement before the majesty of English standards." Although Adams and his peers recognized the decline of the Brahmins' privilege, they could not bring themselves to abdicate.

John I. Taylor

There was one Brahmin, however, who was a fixture at Boston American League games, including the four home games of the 1903 World Series, and he would play an important role in the history of the franchise. John I. Taylor was the son of Civil War general Charles H. Taylor, the Brahmin publisher of the *Boston Globe*. Referred to generally as "John I.," the younger Taylor had tried the newspaper business but showed little interest or talent. His father despaired at the prospects for his son. Baseball, it seemed, was John I.'s only interest. In early 1904, Charles Taylor bought the Boston franchise for his son.

Ballplayers

Ballplayers at the turn of the twentieth century were at the opposite end of the social spectrum from the Brahmin upper class. They were considered a disorderly bunch, untutored and ill-kempt. Mostly sons of working-class fathers, the athletes who played the national game lacked social respectability. A few, however, came from families of moderate means — Rube Marquard's father was the chief engineer of the City of Cleveland; Smoky Joe Wood's father was a Colorado lawyer; and Bill Wambsganss's dad was a Lutheran minister. They were the exceptions rather than the rule. More common were players such as Honus Wagner, who was the son of a Pittsburgh coal miner. Wagner had picked coal himself before escaping to the ball fields. Stan Coveleski, the star Cleveland Indians pitcher during the 1920s, mined coal at age twelve for a nickel an hour, seventy-two hours a week. Although playing ball was "a tough racket," Coveleski told Lawrence Ritter, author of the marvelous oral history *The Glory of Their Times: The Story of the Early Days of Baseball Told by the Men Who Played It,* "I was out of those damn mines for good."

There were a few college men among baseball players—"The Christian Gentleman" Christy Mathewson, "The Peerless Leader" Frank Chance, and "Colby Jack" Coombs stand out in this group—but most players had little formal education. As Sam Crawford states in *The Glory of Their Times*, "We were considered pretty crude." Indeed, they were pretty crude. Some were borderline psychotics, such as Ty Cobb, who was obsessed with the devils in his head and would take out his frustrations on fielders while running the base paths.

Early ballplayers and club management worked hard to promote the respectability of their commercial enterprise, but without much success. Chief Meyers, Mathewson's star catcher with the Giants, explained: "Ballplayers were considered a rowdy bunch. We weren't admitted to hotels, that is, first-class hotels. I guess in a way we were just dumb eggs." Most players were treated poorly by their club owners. On the other hand, as longtime Pittsburgh catcher and manager George Gibson said: "It sure beats hauling bricks!"

Off the field, players drank—mostly beer—and some would arrive for a game inebriated. The saloon and the brothel posed the greatest threats to a ballplayer, and alcoholism and sexually transmitted diseases were the athlete's scourge. The object of adoration on one day, they might be discarded by management the next. It was a tenuous fame.

The Honourables

The 165 guards of the British Honourable Artillery Company arrived in Boston on October 2, 1903, on the steamship *Mayflower*, named after the craft that had carried the Brahmins' forebears to Plymouth Bay in 1620. They were greeted by "an uproarious tooting and wailing of tugboat whistles." Sergeant Fred M. Purport and Lieutenant James M. Usher of the American host committee offered the official greeting: "Welcome, Englishmen!" Upon their arrival, the Honourables paraded for three hours around the city. Their route wound past the Golden Dome of the Massachusetts State House on Beacon Hill, down to the Public Garden and around the Common to City Hall, where Mayor Collins presented the keys of the city to Lord Denbigh and his troops. King Edward wired from Balmoral Castle that he was "delighted to hear of your safe arrival and magnificent reception. Feel certain that you will have a charming visit."

The main event of the Honourables' visit was the gala dinner planned for the new Symphony Hall for Monday evening, October 5. The host organization, the Ancient and Honorable Artillery Company of Massachusetts, Boston's own counterpart to the British Honourables, had provided "the most elaborate electrical and floral decoration ever seen at a dinner in this country." On the Symphony Hall stage, five long tables were set for the British guests. An electric panoply of the English royal crown, synchronized waving flags, and "streamers of soft golden lights" illuminated the hall with reflections of the New Age. High above the stage in bright incandescent bulbs were two dates: "1537," when the British Honourable Artillery Company was chartered, and "1638," when its Massachusetts counterpart was founded. Food for the gala was catered by Alexander C. Nixon of the Algonquin Club of 219 Commonwealth Avenue.

Monday morning's *Boston Globe* offered the following details about that night's Symphony Hall banquet: The fete had cost $60,000 to mount. There were 300 waiters, 75 of whom would pour wine only. There were 10,000 roses, 6,000 yards of laurel, 5,000 chrysanthemum blooms and 100 cases of southern smilax imported from Cuba. Only men were allowed on the dining floor. Ladies would be admitted by ticket to the balcony only. The *Globe* declared that the banquet would set "the world record," without explaining how that was to be determined. The day after, the *Globe* gushed: "There are actually no words to tell of the picture Symphony Hall presented."

Speeches at the gala related with pride the glory and accomplishments of the Anglo-Saxon race, above all others, "producing so many men illustrious as statesmen, philosophers, writers, warriors, inventors and benefactors of mankind," as Harvard professor F. C. De Sumichrast put it in his remarks. He emphasized that Harvard University itself was "a lasting monument to

English interests in America." That night on Huntington Avenue the trinity —the Anglo-Saxon race, the Boston Brahmins, and Harvard College—seemed eternal and omnipotent.

American commercialism was not far away, however. By Thursday morning, October 8, a large advertisement on top of the front page of the *Boston Herald* offered for sale an "Ancient & Honourable SOUVENIR PLATE." The Richard Briggs Company of Boylston Street had produced the plates for the great banquet, but they "held in reserve at the factory a limited number of the superb plates used as souvenirs," and they have been "given permission to dispose of same." The price was set at $5, "and no more will ever be made so that in a short time their value will be priceless."

Across the street from Symphony Hall, a different spectacle had unfolded the prior week, one that would long outlive the insular merriment of the Honourables' pageantry. On the rocky infield and vast outfield of the Huntington Avenue Grounds, the national game had presented the first edition of its annual fall classic. Some notable Brahmins would mix with the masses for that very different celebration.

On Saturday, October 3, 1903, the day after arriving in Boston, the British Honourable Artillery Company, the treasured symbol of all that was English, attended the third game of the first World Series. The Boston hosts had arranged the excursion so their Anglo cousins could experience this American spectacle. Adorned in full dress uniform, the Honourables witnessed the athletic exhibition. According to the *Pittsburgh Press:*

> The Englishmen looked on with amazement at the wild scene of excitement and exuberance. It gave our English cousins a good idea of America's love for outdoor sports, and particularly of our national game of baseball. The hearty applause of the foreign visitors during the game, when any especially brilliant bit of fielding was done, showed that they fully appreciated the beauties of the game.

The coincident visits to Boston's Huntington Avenue Grounds of the British Honourable Artillery Company and the Pittsburgh Pirates illustrate the central role baseball played in the American experience at the turn of the twentieth century. Spectators and participants, Rooters, enthusiasts, and fanactics—those who shared in these events left changed by the experience. Our British relations would take back to England a new appreciation of the vitality of the American spirit. The members of the Pirates baseball club during their sojourn in Boston proved their status as sportsmen of the highest order.

From the earliest days of baseball as a spectator sport, the Brahmins likely appreciated the role of baseball as a needed diversion for the masses, a harmless instrument of social distraction, distinct from the matters of the mind and social policy that had been the Brahmins' inheritance. Certainly, they thought that outside exercise for immigrants in playing or watching the game was better for social development than time spent in saloons or pool halls. They would have agreed with Walter Camp's characterization of the sport in *Century Magazine* in 1889:

> Putting aside for a moment its professional questions, base-ball is for every boy a good, wholesome sport. It brings him out of the close confinement of the schoolroom. It takes the stoop from his shoulders and puts hard, honest muscle all over his frame. It rests his eyes, strengthens his lungs, and teaches him self-reliance and courage.

Most Brahmins would have shied away from immigrant crowds, however. The assertive passions of the newcomers did not mix well with Brahmin reserve. Nevertheless, members of Boston Proper would have been pleased with a uniquely American spectacle—what Camp called "a game for the people"—that held the promise of acculturation so needed in a society that had become increasingly diverse and splintered. They appreciated the pageantry of America's game as a celebration of the new American spirit.

Although most Brahmins were not ready to join the Honoroubles at the Huntington Avenue Grounds, they must have sensed that their time of dominance was ending and their high culture would have to share the attention of the public with more plebeian entertainments. In future years, it would be the attendees at events such as the World Series—for example, John F. Fitzgerald, whose grandson John Fitzgerald Kennedy would be elected president in 1960—who would lead America in the twentieth century.

JOHN F. FITZGERALD

A leader of the famous Boston Royal Rooters,
John "Honey Fitz" Fitzgerald represented his
Boston constituents in Congress and in the
mayor's office. Fitzgerald was always an avid
baseball fan, but his bid to purchase the Boston club
in 1904 was thwarted by American League
president Ban Johnson, who was rightfully
concerned that he could not control Honey Fitz.

4

Boston's Irish Community:
Coming of Age

The greatest fans of the Boston American League club came from the city's large Irish community. Although Mike McGreevey's Royal Rooters were the most visible Irish baseball fanatics, the grandstands at the grounds were filled with the sons and grandsons of Eire. American League president Ban Johnson's plan to hire Jimmy Collins away from the Nationals to lead the new Boston Americans was a brilliant strategy, designed to attract Irish support. Collins then induced the most well-known Irish Beaneater ballplayers—his friends Chick Stahl, Buck Freeman, and Bill Dineen—to cross the railroad tracks over to the American League side and play at the new Huntington Avenue Grounds. It was a matter of enormous pride to the Irish immigrant community to watch fellow countrymen succeed on the ball field.

In the 1880s, Irish fanatics adored Michael Joseph "King" Kelly, the flamboyant outfielder-catcher. A beloved figure on the Chicago White Stockings club, Kelly led the National League in hitting in 1884 (.354) and 1886 (.388). He ran the bases with abandon, inspiring the Maggie Cline song "Slide, Kelly, Slide!" He developed the "Kelly spread," what is now called a hook slide, to offer an infielder only part of a leg to tag. Kelly cut a strikingly handsome figure in his baseball uniform. He was not an angel, however. Kelly's love of women, horses, and liquor was well known. His manager in Chicago, Cap Anson, sent out a detective to report on Kelly's activities. The detective reported that he had observed Kelly drinking lemonade at 3:00 A.M. Anson confronted "Old Kel," who denied the accusation: "It was straight whiskey! I never drank lemonade at that hour in my life!"

Chicago magnate Albert Spalding, the owner of that city's National League franchise, sold the rights to sign Kelly to the Boston National League club after the 1886 season for the astounding price of $10,000 (none of which went to Kelly). The Boston fanatics idolized their new Irish star and bought him two gray horses and a fancy carriage so he could arrive at the ballpark in style. In 1891, they bought him a house. In the off-season, Kelly played vaudeville, starring in the skit "He Would Be an Actor, or The Ball Player's Revenge." Although his ball playing abilities trumped his career as an actor, Kelly never failed to attract an adoring crowd. He was baseball's first superstar.

After the turn of the century, it was Jimmy Collins and his Irish-Catholic teammates who represented Boston, a town the Irish controlled politically. The Irish had come a long way toward American acculturation and, in some ways, now were more "American" than the Brahmins who had retreated from public involvement. The Irish represented the Boston of the twentieth century.

The Migration

Arriving during the mid-nineteenth century from the farming counties of southern and western Ireland, and without the money or experience needed to function in a crowded urban environment, Irish peasants found Boston a forbidding place. Refugees from the potato famine, they did not have the resources to purchase land and start anew as farmers in America. They had come for the short run, confident that they would return to Ireland when the blight had run its course.

Even before the famine, life for peasants in Ireland had been primitive. They rented the land they worked and lived in one-room shanties with thatched roofs. The dominant British landowners secured the peasants' political, social, and legal subjugation, a circumstance that had lasted for generations. The enactment of the Penal Laws in 1695 first prohibited the Irish from practicing their Catholic faith. The Irish could not vote, own land, or attend school. Yet, they had not died of hunger on such a widespread scale before the famine arrived.

The famine destroyed the social and economic life of the old country. The peasants had relied on the potato for food. When in 1845 the blight took hold of the national crop — twenty-first-century DNA research suggests that the origin of the blight was Peruvian bat guano imported into Ireland as fertilizer — famine descended on the land. The blight caused the failure of four seasons of the potato crop. More than a million Irish would starve to death, but more than two million would uproot and travel to the New World. Dublin professor Kevin Whelan, one of Ireland's best known and widely published historians, has suggested that the British saw the blight "as an opportunity for social engineering." John Mitchel wrote in 1861 in *The Last Conquest of Ireland (Perhaps):* "The Almighty indeed sent the potato blight, but the British created the famine." The British thought that potato farming encouraged indolence and overpopulation and wanted to replace potatoes with wheat crops. During the Great Starvation, the British continued to export wheat, oats, barley, butter, eggs, beef, and pork from Ireland in large quantities. The Irish were a troublesome lot in any case, and the British were pleased with the prospect of their exile.

The poorest farmers left first. Unmarried young men or the fathers of a family would pave the way. In desperation, they walked to the western ports, such as Sligo, and boarded the so-called coffin ships, stuffed into steerage as cargo without food and with only two pints of water a day. Disease spread rapidly through the ships. Those who arrived alive after a ten-week journey — the transatlantic death rate was often 30 percent or more — were starving.

Once in Boston, an Irishman would purchase lodging in the house of a countryman or a relative, if he were fortunate. He would look for a work situation in which to earn enough to live. Turning to manual labor or factory work for immediate earnings, the immigrants survived the transplantation.

As the famine continued in the home country, even the previously prosperous farmers took leave of their ancient homeland. They thought that the bogs of Ireland's southern and western counties had been cursed. Counties Cork, Kerry, Galway, and Clare depopulated. With the agricultural base of the Irish economy in shambles, members of the trades and professions who had serviced the farmers' needs followed their example and departed for America. They paid their fare of $20 and rode the Cunard Line to Noodle's Island, the early name given to the sliver of land that was then East Boston. There was no work to do in Ireland. Perhaps Boston could serve as a temporary haven?

Irish Life in Boston

Crammed into two- and three-story tenement housing in the North End and Fort Hill sections of Boston, the new Irish immigrants lived near the mills and wharves where they found work. A Catholic diocese had been established in Boston in 1818, and the new arrivals found friends among co-religionists in this land far from the bogs of Ireland. Although farmers by experience, Irish immigrants clung to the urban environment. Life outside the city would leave them far from the anchor of their lives in America—the Catholic Church.

The North End of Boston, the center of the new Irish settlement, was steeped in Yankee revolutionary history. Samuel Adams, a chief provocateur of the revolution against England, had plotted rebellion in the taverns of the North End. As the most vocal opponent of the British Tea Act, Adams had instigated the legendary Boston Tea Party of December 16, 1773. The new Irish inhabitants of Adams's North End certainly shared his antipathy for British rule.

There was always a need for unskilled laborers on the docks, and the new Irish immigrants eagerly accepted the arduous work. Others peddled fish from the wharves or took factory jobs in the shoe industry. Irish women worked as housekeepers and Irish boys as newsboys, potentially a lucrative trade where they could earn $2.50 a week. Although the Irish made the transition to urban dwellers, they saw their stay in Boston as temporary. They were wrong. They would remain in the Hub and make it their city.

The Irish influx increased Boston's population dramatically by the mid-nineteenth century. In the decade between 1840 and 1850 the city's population swelled from 85,475 to 136,881. In 1847 alone, more than 37,000 immigrants arrived in Boston. By 1855, more than a third of Boston's population was Irish. At the turn of the twentieth century, Boston had become the most Irish city in the world outside of Dublin.

The crowded housing available to the new arrivals offered few comforts. Their homes provided no way to keep food from spoiling, so inhabitants would buy daily supplies from peddlers. The slums were dark and noisy with a fetid odor. Without adequate sewage or drainage, with oppressive heat during the summer and no heat during the winter, life for Irish immigrants was frightful. Disease, particularly among children, was rampant. Cholera caused a ghastly toll, as did tuberculosis, smallpox, and typhus. In the 1870s, one of five Irish infants born in America died before his or her first birthday, and almost an equal number would perish before the age of five.

The Church

From its first settlement by white Europeans, America was predominantly Protestant—a composition of many denominations and sects. Boston was no different, but by mid-nineteenth century the demographics were altered significantly by the heavy influx of Irish immigrants, most of whom were Catholic. The historical tensions and, at times, conflicts between the Protestants and Catholics crossed the Atlantic with them. The Irish were marginalized, hated, and discriminated against for their religious beliefs.

The Catholic Church served a vital role for the Irish immigrants, providing a ballast for those facing urban American life. It served as the tie to folk traditions, to the way of life the Irish had left behind. The Catholic calendar was filled with festival days and ceremonial occasions when the Church provided its flock with an abundance of pleasant and sacred activities. Yet the cohesiveness offered by the Church also fostered insularity. The prevailing Protestant ethos reinforced this separateness by systematically excluding the Irish from avenues of economic opportunity. The popular ad or storefront sign read "NINA," well understood to mean "No Irish Need Apply."

Protestant preachers, such as Lyman Beecher of Boston's Hanover Street Church, warned their congregants as early as the 1830s against the evils of the Catholic invasion:

> Three-fourths of the foreign emigrants whose accumulating tide is rolling in upon us, are, through the medium of their religion and priesthood, entirely accessible to the control of the potentates of Europe, as if they were an army of soldiers, enlisted and officered, and spreading through the land.

As a result of the push-pull of discrimination—pushed into isolation, pulled toward the Church and a large, welcoming immigrant community—full participation in American secular life would take generations for the Irish. The church building itself provided a sacred and quiet space where one could escape the squalor and disharmony of the slums. The first Catholic church in the North End, St. Mary's of the Sacred Heart, was built in 1834. It was a spacious facility, bright and clean, everything the immigrants' homes were not. The prospect of eternal salvation offered by the Church also ameliorated the unpleasant circumstances of daily life. The Irish immigrant adopted a passive philosophy of acceptance and opposed political reform. If life in this world was only a way station to everlasting glory in the next, the harsh realities of everyday existence were merely transitory.

The public schools of Boston—the first in the nation—were under Protestant domination, and Catholic children and their religion were subject to scorn and ridicule. As the Irish population grew, the Church began to operate a separate system of parochial schools. Eventually, half of all Catholic students attended schools under the Church's aegis. After school, children would play on the streets of the slums or on the tenement rooftops. They made up games and played homemade versions of baseball in the alleyways to avoid the ever-present challenges of street traffic and trolley car tracks. By age fourteen, most children were forced to quit school and go to work.

The Snowball Fights

Irish and Brahmin youngsters lived separate lives. Even those Irish children who attended public schools because their families could not afford the cost of parochial education did not study with the social elite, who had long departed public education for private academies. The Irish, of course, did not attend Harvard.

Curiously, there was one place and one time when the Irish and Brahmin youngsters would meet, and it became a ritual of fabled importance. Each winter, as the snow accumulated on Boston Common, boys from both communities would prepare for the celebrated snowball fights.

In his autobiography *The Education of Henry Adams,* Adams related stories of these annual snowball games of war. On one side were the "Beacon Hillers," the progenies of the scions of Boston. Dressed in the finest clothes of the day—wool suits, stockings, collars, and caps—they faced a shabby contingent of Irish North Enders, attired in baggy coats and worn pants. (Adams called them "roughs and young blackguards.") Here class conflict was played out with flying snowballs. Adams accused the townies of spiking their snowballs with rocks, one of which hit Henry Higginson, "Bully Hig" as he was called by his fellows; he was led off the field bleeding. The snowball fights would rage all day and into dusk. Many Brahmins would later recall these fights as the high point of their adolescent years. When the contests were over, both sides retreated to their separate enclaves.

Gambling

Almost from its inception, baseball offered spectators and participants alike an opportunity to gamble. Baseball did not invent gambling, of course. Betting was an ancient pastime. The mythological Roman gods Zeus, Hades, and Poseidon were said to have split the universe by a throw of dice, thereby allocating exclusive territorial rights to heaven, hell, and the sea. The Old Testament relates that Moses used a lottery to award lands west of the Jordan River. Greek and Roman nobles played games of chance. During the Middle Ages, gambling spread beyond the social elites to the common folk.

In the Massachusetts Bay colony, the Puritans outlawed gambling, along with the possession of cards, dice, and gaming tables. Most English colonists, however, accepted gambling as an innocent diversion, and the colonies used lotteries as a source of funds. (In fact, the proceeds of a lottery in Massachusetts were used to support the establishment of Harvard College in the seventeenth century and the rebuilding of Boston's Faneuil Hall in the eighteenth century.) Wagering on sports first began with betting on the outcome of horse races, a practice dating from the early nineteenth century. Periodically outlawed as a social ill, gambling persisted out of the public view only to reemerge after the public tired of its prohibition.

Betting on the outcome of baseball games was an accepted part of the commercial amusement almost from its inception. Although betting was not limited to the Irish, some of the most prominent of Boston's "sports" were sons and grandsons of Eire.

In 1871, with the arrival in Boston of George Wright's Red Stockings, the local newspapers began reporting betting odds on game outcomes. After Boston's first game against the Washington Olympics on May 5, 1871, the *Boston Herald* reported that "it is understood in sporting circles that a heavy pile of lucre changed hands because of the results." Within a very short time, it became well accepted that players, managers, and owners would bet on the games, although it was never reported that they bet against their own clubs. Open betting prevailed in the grandstands at ball games, typically along the third-base line. Cap Anson, one of the game's best-known players during his twenty-two-year career, 1876–1897, openly placed bets on his White Stockings club to win. Manager John Montgomery Ward won twenty shares of Giants stock in 1892 from club director Edward Talcott based on his prediction of where the Giants club would finish that season. (It finished eighth in the twelve-team circuit.) Although the magnates of the game sought respectability for their sports enterprise, that goal was difficult to achieve within an atmosphere of gambling, although Baltimore's James Cardinal Gibbons thought baseball a wholesome enterprise played by "exemplary young men whose moral rectitude of character is above reproach." Not all community leaders agreed. In 1887, Pittsburgh judge J. W. F. White lectured a defendant in a larceny case about the inherent dangers of baseball: "You should never go to a ball game. A majority of the persons connected with base ball bet on the results of the games, and all betting is gambling. Base ball is one of the evils of the day."

The club owners themselves were among the most open and notorious gamblers. They would wager among themselves on the result of games or the outcome of the pennant races. They would wager with their players. On Saturday, October 3, 1903, the day of the third game of the World Series, Boston newspapers reported that the local police had answered a call to break up a crap game in the North End. They arrested seven young men, most locals of the North End, who had rolled the dice on the same sidewalk each Saturday for months. The police had finally answered the complaints of tradesmen, pedestrians, and churchgoers to stem the practice. The police confiscated two sets of "bones" (dice). Apparently, no one saw the irony that the report of the bust appeared on the same page as the stories of open gambling on the World Series. At least $50,000 would be wagered on the first World Series.

One foreseeable byproduct of gambling on sporting events was the blatant opportunity to arrange the outcome of contests. In 1867, long before the advent of organized professional leagues, *Harper's Weekly* denounced the "common . . . tricks by which games have been 'sold' for the benefits of the gamblers." Professional leagues understood this risk, and for more than a century the possibility of a fixed game would bedevil the sport of baseball. The prospect of being able to wager attracted interest, but the specter that the contest might not be on the level diminished both interest and wagering. Players were not above "hippodroming," as fixing a game was called. In order to discourage throwing games, club owners had to pay their players an adequate salary so they could ignore gamblers' entreaties, and at the turn of the twentieth century the owners were not yet ready to do so.

Of course, the official rules of the various leagues prohibited such player misconduct. The National Association, the earliest circuit, had an edict that read, "no person engaged in a match, either as umpire, scorer or player, shall be either directly or indirectly interested in any bet upon the game." The rule was later amended to mandate expulsion from the association for those engaged in such prohibited conduct. In 1875, the last year of its existence, the National Association suffered repeated betting and fixing scandals, including one instance where crooked players for Philadelphia took payoffs from a rival group of gamblers, double-crossing their original benefactors.

As early as the second season of the National League, the leaders of that circuit vowed to take a strong stand against gambling and the possibility of a fix. The Louisville club was in first place in August 1877 when it lost eight straight games. Rumors of foul play were in the air, and club owner Charles Chase investigated. Four players, including his star pitcher, Art Devlin, and the club's best hitter, George Hall, confessed to the perfidy. Chase suspended the four offenders, and the league upheld the suspensions and converted them to lifetime expulsions from the organized professional game. This strong medicine provided only a temporary cure, however. In 1882, for example, umpire Richard Higham was banned from baseball for telling gamblers how to bet on the games he was officiating.

Glenn Stout and Richard A. Johnson in their superb history, *Red Sox Century*, claim that the Boston Americans threw the first game of the 1903 World Series. They point the finger at catcher Lou Criger, who made four questionable plays that day. Freeman and Ferris each contributed two mis-plays. Stout and Johnson even suggest that Cy Young was in on the fix.

It is true that it was not unusual at that time for professional games to be "arranged," and the players certainly had a motive to extend the length of the Series. Their pay was based on the total gate receipts for all the Se-ries games combined. Twenty years later, Criger signed an affidavit stating that he had been offered $12,000 to throw the Series, but he swore he had rejected the offer.

There are problems with the inference Stout and Johnson draw. If the players were going to throw a game to extend the Series, why would it be the first contest? That loss did not extend the Series. If the players wanted to extend the Series, why did the Series end at eight games and not its full nine? And what gamblers benefited from the first game loss? The newspaper reports were filled with stories of wagers made, or offered by, Boston fanatics on a first-game victory, and the Pittsburgh "sports" seemed unwilling to place bets until they saw the clubs play each other. Frankly, it seems contrary to character for Cy Young to be involved in such disrepu-table activity.

Baseball's illicit relationship with gambling would reach its nadir in the early 1920s with the revelation that the Chicago White Sox had thrown the 1919 World Series. Boston's Joseph "Sport" Sullivan, an original member of the glorious Royal Rooters of 1903, was the instigator of that fix, backed by the money of New York gambler Arnold Rothstein. The newspapers in 1903 had regaled Sullivan for his courageous bets for the Americans. Two decades later, he was the scourge of the game.

Mike "Nuf Ced" McGreevey

The most memorable character involved in the 1903 baseball pageantry was a five-foot mustachioed barkeep named Michael McGreevey. His Columbus Avenue Third Base Saloon became part of Boston's baseball legend along with Cy Young and Jimmy Collins. Dressed in his dark Sunday-best suit with a high stiff white collar and a black bowler hat, McGreevey would lead the World Series march of Royal Rooters to Boston's Huntington Avenue Grounds and to Exposition Park in Pittsburgh.

McGreevey was a ubiquitous presence at the World Series. He danced an Irish reel on the metal roof above the Americans' bench, leading his Royal Rooters in song and cheers. His fellow Irish Rooters were also well established in the Boston community and widely known as "sporting men," that is, gamblers. Charles Lavis, often mentioned in the press as another leader of the Royal Rooters, owned a saloon, bowling alleys, and a hotel at the corner of Harvard and Washington Streets in Boston. Charley Young, an accountant by trade, was the official scorer of two candlepin bowling leagues in Boston. Charles Green owned a large wholesale grocery outfit. John C. L. Sheafe ran a downtown bowling alley located next door to the Colonial Theatre, and W. G. Ferris owned lanes in Roslindale and Quincy. C. W. Smith was a druggist from nearby Medford. He claimed to have missed only three baseball games in six seasons. John Keenan owned a "sporting" saloon on Howard Street in downtown Boston.

McGreevey's prominent role in the social history of the 1903 World Series is based not only on his leadership of the Royal Rooters, but also on his proprietorship of the Third Base Saloon. The neighborhood saloons of Boston provided immigrant workingmen—especially the dominant Irish male population—with a safe and welcoming social space. These establishments were clean, well lit, and warm in the winter. They offered a meeting place not unlike a social club, where men could swap stories, enjoy spirits, and laugh and sing. In one twelve-block area of the North End, there were 540 establishments that served liquor, including grocery stores that converted into saloons at night.

For regular patrons, saloons were a semipublic accommodation in which they shared a sense of ownership and belonging, not unlike a ballpark. Although leisure time was minimal, saloon owners captured that commercial opportunity by providing the social gathering spot laborers needed. The saloon became a place for the discussion of politics and baseball, part of the culture of the big city. Irish men generally favored hard liquor. German immigrants, on the other hand, preferred their nickel beer. Saloons provided sustenance and safety in the neighborhoods. At a time when water was not potable and milk was suspect as well, the only safe drinks were spirits and beer.

The saloon keeper was often a public figure, like Mike McGreevey. A small businessman faced with an abundance of competition, the entrepreneur worked hard to attract steady patrons and keep them loyal to his establishment. Offering a free lunch table and a refuge from the travails of work and home life, saloons especially prospered when they could claim distinction as, for example, the home base of the Royal Rooters.

Although it is easy to rhapsodize about the role played by ethnic saloons, they also had a significant negative influence on society. Some workingmen would spend all their meager wages to imbibe while their families went hungry. Intoxicated husbands returning home late at night might abuse their wives. Also a breeding ground for corrupt politicians, criminals, and juvenile delinquents, the saloons were not a benign influence on immigrant society. Periodically regulated by public authorities and later unionized, the neighborhood saloons thrived as an urban institution until banned by Prohibition in the early 1920s.

Politics and "Honey Fitz"

In the late nineteenth century, the second generation of the Irish immigrant community had four main career paths. They could pursue government employment, mainly police work. They could study for the priesthood. They could try their hand at professional sports, such as baseball or boxing. Or they could aspire to party politics and run for political office. By the end of the century, it was apparent to all observers, as a reporter for the *Pittsburgh Dispatch* wrote, that "the Irish run Boston." The Brahmins' "noble families" were "fading and faded scions." The storied career of John F. Fitzgerald exemplified the rise of the Boston Irish politician and the intertwining of politics and baseball.

John Francis Fitzgerald, the son of an immigrant fish peddler, was born on Ferry Street in Boston's North End in 1863. His parents, Thomas and Rosanna Fitzgerald, had arrived in America from Bruff, County Limerick, with the second wave of Irish farmers. Young Johnny Fitzgerald, the fourth son in a family that would produce ten boys (two sisters died quite young) attended public school. (The Church had not yet established its parochial school system.) In 1879, after his wife died, Thomas Fitzgerald vowed that one of his sons would become a doctor. Johnny was picked to fulfill his father's dreams. He attended Boston Latin School and was admitted to Harvard Medical School in 1884.

Boston Latin became a public high school in 1835, although it traces its origins back to the earliest days of settlement. Distinguished graduates included Cotton Mather (1669), Benjamin Franklin (1714), Samuel Adams (1729), and John Hancock (1745). It was originally a Yankee preserve, but by 1879 the Brahmins had established their own elite preparatory schools, leaving Boston Latin with a diverse student population that included the Irish, Jews, and Yankees. At school, Fitzgerald honed his public speaking and debating skills, which would prove valuable later in his life when he pursued public office.

Before John Fitzgerald could complete his first year of medical school, however, Thomas Fitzgerald died of pneumonia, leaving his family without a source of income. Although Thomas had wanted his son to complete medical school, the young Fitzgerald decided he had to bear the responsibility for the family. He visited the neighborhood Democratic ward boss, Matthew Keany, who hired him as an apprentice. A ward boss distributed favors to immigrant families in exchange for the promise of their loyalty at the polls. Machine politics controlled the democratic process, and Fitzgerald was an avid student, progressing through the machine system. As Robert A. Woods wrote in 1903:

> Ward politics is largely an affair of young men. It brings them into some sort of equal association with persons of influence and power. Ambitious youths, with no one to help them to a profes-

sional or commercial career, and having prejudices to meet in those lines against their race and religion, find an open, inviting opportunity in politics.

There was much positive work for a ward boss to accomplish in serving his Irish constituency, as Woods described:

> He has an endless number of thankless tasks laid upon him. He must see that this poor family's rent is paid; he must secure legal assistance for that oppressed immigrant; he has to arbitrate local disputes; he must secure for the sick admission to the hospital; he is pressed to use his best endeavors to get ambitious but incapable girls into the high or normal school; he must find places for them as stenographers or teachers when they have finished their education; he must put the poor, worthy and unworthy alike, in the way of receiving help from church or municipal charities; he is besieged for opportunities of work by widows and helpless people.

Boss Keany designated Fitzgerald a "ward healer," a member of the party's speakers' bureau, and finally a "shock trooper," whose responsibility it was to disrupt political meetings of the opposition through spirited heckling. Fitzgerald relished these tasks and performed them splendidly. Eventually, he rose to a clerk's position in the Custom House, earning $1,500 a year, a substantial income for the times. He earned the nickname "Little Fitzie," later changed to the more familiar "Honey Fitz," as his political successes accumulated.

Fitzgerald soon turned his attention to a career in elected office, first running successfully for Boston's Common Council. He kept close to his political base in the Irish neighborhood, participating in a variety of fraternal organizations and delivering a city-funded park to the North End. When Boss Keany died in 1892, Fitzgerald assumed his role, then ran for state senate (bypassing the usual steps of running for board of aldermen and the state house of representatives). He cast his lot on Beacon Hill with the progressives who represented the poor and jobless, addressing the social needs of the urban communities. Fitzgerald supported minimum wage legislation ($2.00 a day) and maximum hour work limits for women and children. In 1894, at the height of the economic depression of the late nineteenth century, Fitzgerald ran for a seat in U.S. Congress as the cheerful and irrepressible "boy candidate." Much like politicians today who call for term limits, his rallying cry was "The people believe in rotation."

Fitzgerald held his congressional office for three terms, and he was well regarded by his fellow Democrats. He led the fight against immigration restrictions promoted by the Republicans and, in particular, by Boston Brahmin senator Henry Cabot Lodge. Responding to Lodge's question "Do you think the Jews or the Italians have any right in this country?" Fitzgerald retorted that those immigrants "have as much right as your father or mine. After all, it was only a difference of a few ships."

By 1884, Hugh O'Brien had been elected the first Irish mayor of Boston, and the Irish had taken control of local politics. In 1900, having served three terms in Congress, Fitzgerald was "rotated out." He again turned his attention to local politics, aspiring to the patronage-laden job of mayor for the City of Boston. That year, however, the party bosses favored Patrick A. Collins for mayor instead of Fitzgerald.

Fitzgerald would have to wait his turn, and he did. Finally he won City Hall in 1905 after Collins's death. Fitzgerald's followers praised him as a loyal churchman and public servant. His opponents labeled him the "Napoleon of the North End."

Like many of his countrymen, Fitzgerald was an avid baseball fan and an active and visible leader of the Royal Rooters. He continued to build up his base among his fellow Irish while broadening his appeal to all voters as a "reformer." He also purchased a Catholic weekly newspaper, the *Republic*, which became a platform for his views. Fitzgerald turned the struggling newspaper into a financial success that was read throughout the Irish community. With his earnings from the *Republic*, a net of $25,000 a year, Fitzgerald even made a bid to purchase the Boston American League baseball club

from Henry Killilea in 1904. However, league president Ban Johnson vetoed the sale to Fitzgerald. Johnson would countenance only owners he
could control, and Honey Fitz certainly did not fit into that category.

The Third Game

McGreevey, Lavis, and Fitzgerald led the parade of loyal Irish fanatics into
the Huntington Avenue Grounds on Saturday, October 3, for the third game
of the World Series. The Royal Rooters marched across the field behind the
Letter Carriers' Brass Band they had hired for the occasion. Each rooter
carried an American flag and wore a blue and gold badge on the lapel of
his Sunday-best coat.

Boston's faithful turned out in considerable numbers for this memorable third contest at the Huntington Avenue Grounds. The fanatics had
been cheered by the hometown victory in game two. Game three took place
on a Saturday afternoon, when most people were not at work. By noon,
the trolley "cars to the game began to arrive at the grounds, creaking and
groaning under the loads of enthusiastic human freight." Speculators
sold $1 grandstand tickets for as high as $10, which the *Boston Globe* called
"grand opera prices." Thousands of men, women, and children struggled
madly to gain entrance to the overfilled stadium as trolley car after trolley
car rolled up Huntington Avenue. Walter Smith, the assistant secretary of
the Pittsburgh club, was drafted to work in the Boston ticket booth.

Thousands of eager fanatics walked down Massachusetts Avenue from
Cambridge and, from the other direction, the South End. Special trains
brought thousands more from Springfield, Worcester, Providence, Port-
land, and Manchester. "Baseball crazy, the late comers were not to be denied." Two women stumbled in the crowd and had to be hospitalized after
being stomped on by the onrushing multitudes. The *Pittsburgh Press* reported that "for a time it looked as if someone would be killed in the crush."

Paid attendance that day was recorded as 18,801, the high point of
the Series, but many more simply scaled the outfield walls, some with the
help of ropes lowered by friends from the center-field bleachers. Probably

upwards of 25,000 attended, and another 10,000 were turned away. Every inch of wall space was taken: "At a quarter before 2:00 the fence from bleacher end to bleacher end served as a perch for thousands. The bipeds without feathers on the fence top were packed as closely as prisoners in lockstep formation." The "surging, struggling mass" of fans would not be denied. Crowds poured into the outfield behind ropes that could not restrain their wild enthusiasm. Their numbers continued to build. "There was a tooting of horns and a clamor of voices, mingled with the calls of peanut and score-card boys."

At 2:00 P.M., an hour before the start of the contest, the outfield ropes gave way before the surging crowd. Fans stampeded toward the diamond, intent on watching their heroes toss the ball around in infield practice. They stopped barely three feet from the base paths. Captains Collins and Clarke of the respective squads considered calling the game unless the crowd could be lassoed behind a restraint. The police contingent on hand was inadequate to control the crowd and "gave itself over, chiefly, to rescuing women who were caught in the crush."

Police called for reinforcements from headquarters at Pemberton Square and pulled their clubs, but did not use them. The Boston team's business manager, Joe Smart, and his assistants, armed with bats, began to push the crowd off the infield. Coats were ripped and hats lost in the fray. At fifteen minutes before the appointed hour, however, the crowd remained firmly entrenched on the outfield grass directly behind the infield.

Some in the throng remembered similar "remarkable attendances" in Boston's baseball history. At one game in 1876, an immense crowd turned out to see the first meeting between the Boston Nationals and the Chicago White Stockings. The prior year, William Hulbert, owner of the Chicago team, had signed away four premier Boston players to play the inaugural season of the new National League with the Chicago entry. The crowd broke down the fences at the South End Grounds to witness the return of their old heroes. Another, younger group of fans remembered a similar onslaught for opening day of the Players League season at the Columbus Avenue Grounds in 1890. Although these earlier contests in Boston had attracted large crowds, nothing approached the throng of humanity who had come to witness the pivotal third game.

Extra police arrived at the scene with a new strategy and the instruments to carry it out—long pieces of rubber hose secured by four men on each end. The crowd slowly released its grip on the diamond. "Inch by inch, the swaying mass fell back, and with each backward step the police gained hope [and were] spurred on to greater endeavors." By shortly after 3:00 P.M. the game could commence, although the crowd was little more than two hundred feet from home plate. The crowd in front of the grandstand and bleachers stood twenty persons deep. The peanut and scorecard boys made a fortune that day selling wooden boxes at a dollar each for those in the outfield crowd to stand on so that they could peer over others' heads and watch the contest.

Pittsburgh captain Fred Clarke and Boston captain Jimmy Collins agreed that any ball hit fair into the crowd either on the fly or on the ground would be a double. It was a rule that would cost the Boston club the contest.

Pittsburgh's Deacon Phillippe, the "illusive ball tosser," returned to the mound for the Pirates on one day's rest and gave up only two runs to the Boston nine. Long Tom Hughes started the contest for the Americans. After retiring the first five batters, Hughes appeared rattled when Ritchey's pop fly to short center fell into the crowd for a ground-rule double. Had the crowd been farther back, the bloop hit would have been easily caught. This was the first of the Pittsburgh "fungoes" that fell into the crowd for ground-rule doubles.

Hughes walked the next batter, then Phelps stroked a single to center, scoring Pittsburgh's first tally. In the third inning, Hughes allowed the first three batters to reach safely, and one scored on a sharply hit single by Leach. Boston captain Collins sent Cy Young behind the stands to warm up. (Not scheduled to pitch, Young had been working in the club office in his street clothes counting the proceeds of the ticket sales.) The *Post* reported: "A murmur of apprehension let Hughes know unmistakably that the crowd were as anxious as himself."

Now prepared to face the Nationals, Young forced his way through the crowd of spectators to relieve Hughes, and the crowd greeted him warmly: "En masse the people arose and yelled approval." He proceeded to wing Wagner on the shoulder with a "speedy inshoot" that made the Pittsburgh star's face "crinkle like an old ash dump boot." One more run would score on an infield out before the inning ended when the daring Wagner made the final out, caught in a rundown between third and home. Although Young would pitch scoreless ball until Pittsburgh scored a single tally in the eighth on two fielding errors, the Boston batters had managed a total of only two runs.

The press reported that the day was filled with bad luck. The *Boston Globe* claimed that a ground-rule double hit by Boston's Candy Lachance that fell deep into the massive crowd on the field would likely have been an inside-the-park home run on a clear field. Both the *Herald* and the *Press* were more emphatic, claiming that the throng had defeated the locals. No one bothered to mention that the throng and the ground rules were the same for the American batters as they were for the Nationals.

Unknown to those in attendance, there was good fortune that day that saved the national pastime from an enormous tragedy. The *Herald* reported two days later that two late arrivals at the game, Jerry MacKay and Frank Rose, while searching under the wooden third-base stands for boxes to stand on so they could see the contest, came upon an out-of-control roaring fire. While Rose stomped on the flames, MacKay "hastened to the tonic stand and soon returned with buckets of water with which to extinguish the blaze." Their quick action prevented a conflagration that could have cost thousands of lives in the packed wooden stadium.

In less than two hours, the Pirates had bested Boston 4–2 and assumed a two games to one lead in the Series. Eighteen telegraph wires running from the Grounds reported the results to fifty afternoon newspapers across the country. Pittsburgh owner Barney Dreyfuss commented to a reporter from the *Herald:* "I told you so." Manager Collins announced after the game that from then on he would rely only on Young and Dineen to pitch the Boston club to victory.

GAME 3

Team	1	2	3	4	5	6	7	8	9	R	H	E
Pittsburgh	0	1	2	0	0	0	0	1	0	4	7	1
Boston	0	0	0	1	0	0	0	1	0	2	4	2

The teams headed west to Pittsburgh for the next four scheduled games. The National League's dominance over the upstart American League champions seemed evident, but the Boston faithful were not ready to concede. The clubs still looked as evenly matched, the *Globe* reported, "as two red hackles pecking corn." Filled with the Boston ball club and officials, and 125 Royal Rooters, the train was scheduled to leave South Station for Pittsburgh at 10:15 A.M. sharp the next morning.

EXPOSITION PARK

*Located on the floodplain north of the
Allegheny River, Exposition Park was the site
of the four Pittsburgh games of the first World
Series. Across from the park on the Pittsburgh
riverfront, steel mills blackened the sky over
the Smoky City.*

5

The Series Heads West to the Smoky City

With the Pirates leading the Series two games to one, the postseason tournament shifted six hundred miles west to Pittsburgh, known as the Smoky City. The next four contests were scheduled for the Pirates' Exposition Park, if all four games were necessary for the Pittsburgh club to total five wins and prevail in the Series. No one really expected that a return trip to Boston would be necessary. The Pirates had already demonstrated their dominance over the Americans on Boston's home turf. The fourth game would reconfirm the general expectation that the Pirates would rule the baseball world as the first champions of the major leagues.

On Sunday morning, October 4, 1903, the Royal Rooters, more than one hundred strong, boarded the train at South Station in Boston and departed west for Pittsburgh a half-hour late at 10:45 A.M. They each had paid their fare of $20 for the round-trip travel on the Boston & Albany line. Hundreds of well-wishers were on the platform to bid them farewell, including Ivers W. Adams, the president of the 1876 Boston National League team. Accompanying the enthusiastic Rooters was Major J. J. McNamara, a veteran of the Civil War, who "looks and acts as lively as many of the younger men in the party." (A reporter for the *Boston Globe* recalled an incident in

1874 when McNamara, a Boston policeman after the war, protected an umpire from attack by an angry and disappointed Boston crowd after Philadelphia bested the Wright brothers' Boston Red Stockings in a National Association baseball game.)

Two of the Americans' ballplayers, Charley Farrell and George Lachance, boarded the westbound train with the Rooters at South Station. (Mrs. Lachance accompanied her husband on the trip.) The train stopped first at the Trinity Place station near Copley Square to board manager Jimmy Collins and the remainder of his squad: "The men," a reporter recalled, "appeared to be in fine condition and in the best of spirits." The train proceeded west the length of Massachusetts, then through Albany and on to Syracuse, where hurler Bill Dineen's friends showed up to wish him and his teammates luck in the Series. At the next stop, the city fathers of Buffalo promised captain Jimmy Collins, a native son, the keys to the city if the Americans prevailed. The *Boston Post* reported: "Sleep, except for the players, was out of the question." The train was due in Pittsburgh, "the land of perpetual smoke," by early Monday morning.

The train arrived in a rainy Pittsburgh two hours late on October 5, 1903. The Boston players and their supporters checked into the Monongahela House Hotel, Pittsburgh's most famous landmark, where they would reside during their western sojourn. (President Lincoln had stayed at the Monongahela House on the way to his first inaugural in 1861. Presidents Grant, Cleveland, and the recently martyred McKinley had also stayed at the Monongahela.) The players were surprised at the hotel by the unexpected arrival of Hugh Duffy, the popular and esteemed captain of the Boston Beaneaters of the 1890s. (Duffy's .438 batting average in 1894 remains baseball's individual season record. After his magnificent 1894 season, Duffy received a raise from the Beaneaters of $12.50 a month.) Duffy was on his way east from Milwaukee, where he managed a minor league team, and he had stopped off in Pittsburgh to lift the spirits of the Hub's finest.

The Pirates club and its small band of rooters had taken an earlier train home to Pittsburgh and were greeted by a crowd of five thousand supporters at Union Station. It was a "great and noisy reception," said the *Herald*.

Deacon Phillippe, the winning pitcher in the Pirates' two Series victories, reported that he was much fatigued from his successful outing the prior Saturday: "We had to keep pegging away. It was rather wearing." At the train station, Honus Wagner quickly caught a local train home to Carnegie, Pennsylvania, a suburb of the Smoky City.

Both teams could use a rest, and fortunately for them the first game in Pittsburgh, scheduled for the afternoon of the day the clubs arrived, would be postponed. Rain had been falling continuously, and the outfield resembled "an inland sea." Pirate manager Fred Clarke declared that Exposition Park, the Pirates' field on the north shore of the Allegheny River, was too muddy and thus unfit for play. Jimmy Collins commented to the Boston press that this was more bad luck for the Americans. It would give the Pirates' star hurler Deacon Phillippe an extra day of rest.

Patsy Dougherty, the Boston's left fielder, spent the day visiting friends in Homestead, the steel town just outside Pittsburgh where he had played minor league ball. Most of the players and club officials of both teams attended the opening of the Orpheum Show that night at the Duquesne Theatre as the guests of management. The performance included a "clever pair of comedians," McIntyre and Heath, doing two of their minstrel sketches, "On Guard" and "The Man from Montana," as well as Merian's troop of trained dogs.

The delay did not chill the enthusiasm of the Boston Royal Rooters, however, who took to singing and parading through the Pittsburgh streets, "their red badges bidding defiance to the Pittsburgh supporters." (The local newspapers referred to the visitors from Boston as "the cultured crowd" or the "fanatics" from the "city of learning.") Despite the two losses for their beloved Boston nine, they were "not at all downcast." Their badges were made of red silk attached by a gold pin with the inscription "Boston American League Rooters, 1903." Traffic stalled downtown on Smithfield Street as onlookers watched the parade of the Boston faithful.

The Royal Rooters hired a local fifty-piece Italian band to help with the rooting at the game the next day and to entertain later at the Monongahela House—win or lose. Fortuitously, that afternoon one Rooter visited a

Pittsburgh music store seeking appropriate music for the Boston loyalists to sing during the games to come. He selected a song called "Tessie," composed by Will R. Anderson for John C. Fisher's new "stupendous production," *The Silver Slipper.* It would become the celebrated theme song of the Royal Rooters:

> Tessie, you make me feel so badly.
> Why don't you turn around.
> Tessie, you know I love you madly.
> Babe, my heart weighs about a pound.
> Don't blame me if I ever doubt you.
> You know I couldn't live without you.
> Tessie, you are my only, only, only.

As the rain continued to fall in Pittsburgh, the Rooters devised parodies to the Tessie song that would bolster the spirits of the Boston players and annoy both the Pittsburgh baseball players and their fans.

Pittsburgh owner Barney Dreyfuss resolved to prevent a repeat of the uncontrolled overflow of spectators that had jeopardized the third game the prior Saturday in Boston. He made a deal with a local circus and hired their workers to erect eighteen hundred additional "circus seats" in front of the grandstand at Exposition Park to accommodate the expected large crowd for the contest the next day. He also requested extra police from the authorities.

Ticket prices were set at 50¢ for general admission, 75¢ for the grandstand, and $1 for the box seats. There were sixty-five boxes with eight seats in each, all of which had already been sold for the entire Series. William Chase Temple, former owner of the Pirates and a wealthy businessman, had purchased three boxes for the Series. Temple also sent Dreyfuss a check for $100 to be distributed among the Pirate players to show his appreciation for their fine work in Boston. Temple was a great sportsman. He had purchased the silver Temple Cup that symbolized preeminence in the National League in the 1890s. According to the official National Football League chronology, in 1900 Temple became the first individual owner of a professional football team, the Duquesne Country and Athletic Club.

President Dreyfuss purchased twenty-five extra tickets for the personal friends he had invited to join him at the park. Spectators were expected to arrive from as far away as Cleveland for the festivities. "The people here," reported the *Pittsburgh Press,* "are baseball crazy."

Pittsburgh's Economic Geography

Settled at a crossroads of the expanding American nation, Pittsburgh is located at the confluence of two great rivers, the Allegheny and the Mononga-hela, that formed the Ohio River, the avenue to the frontier in the days before rails and roads. A thousand miles downriver, the Ohio joins the Mississippi. While serving as a British colonial officer, George Washington had chosen the "Forks of the Ohio" as "well situated for a fort," and Fort Pitt, named in honor of the British prime minister, became the strategic bulwark of the western frontier. A village grew up around the fort and numbered some 150 inhabitants by 1760. By the end of the century, the town, now referred to as Pittsburgh, claimed 300 citizens, mostly farmers, traders, and artisans.

In the nineteenth century, Pittsburgh provided the departure point for those who would settle the fertile lands to the west. Local craftsmen built flatboats to transport people downriver and keelboats that could travel the river in both directions. Industries soon prospered in Pittsburgh, first glass manufacturing and then ironworks that would provide the raw material for the metal railroad ribbons that would crisscross the nation. By mid-nineteenth century, the expansion of the railroads assured easy access over the mountains from the east, and Pittsburgh had became the leading city of the region.

Pittsburgh's appellation as the Smoky City was well deserved. Coal and coke powered the town's manufacturing, steamboats, and household heat-ing. Tons of coal were mined locally and moved by barge and boxcar to factories that belched black soot so dense that often sunlight was blocked out of the sky. In an article in *Atlantic Monthly* in 1901, William Lucien Scaife explained Pittsburgh's "real meaning and mission, namely the conquest of nature by intelligent energy directing suitable machinery, whose life comes from that smoke and dirt producer, bituminous coal."

Pittsburgh's environment was toxic, its rivers polluted and its streets filled with raw sewage and household waste. It was well described as "hell with the lid taken off." Epidemics of cholera and typhoid fever were the price paid for "the incredibly rapid transformation of a savage wilderness into the iron, steel and glass centre of the world." The local Pittsburgh newspapers were proud to draw the distinction between their blue-collar, hardworking town and the "City of Culture," as they referred to Boston. Pittsburgh was an industrial city.

Pittsburgh's smoke even affected baseball games. In 1899, in one National League game between the Pirates and the Louisville Colonels, the visitors scored four runs in the top of the ninth inning to take a 6–5 lead. Before the Pirates could complete the bottom of the ninth inning, however, heavy black smoke from the steel mills blanketed Exposition Park, blotting out the sunlight. The umpire was forced to call the game, and, in accordance with the rules, the score reverted to the prior completed inning. As a result, the Pirates were victorious by a score of 5–2.

In 1875, a Scottish immigrant turned entrepreneur, Andrew Carnegie, had opened the Edgar Thomson Works at Braddock, the first plant to produce cheap steel in the Pittsburgh region. Called the "Great Ironmaster" by local newspapers, Carnegie was exalted as an example of the limitless potential of immigrants. He and his business cohorts built steel mills in the floodplains, and their blast furnaces, foundries, rolling mills, and machine shops became the engines of American industrial progress. Steel production added jobs and wealth, supplementing the established iron and glass industries that had made Pittsburgh's industrial reputation. Abutting the mills were abundant sources of energy, in particular coal that could be mined from the surface. Industrial suburbs spread along the Monongahela River. Carnegie became one of the richest men in the world, although he regularly espoused the virtues of poverty in developing character: "It is the mind that makes the body rich." It was steel that made Carnegie rich.

Only a few men in Pittsburgh enjoyed the prosperity of the time. Those who actually produced the industrial products, the workers in the mills, lived squalid lives. They worked dangerous, long days of dreary repetition. "Workers," the *National Labor Tribune* wrote in 1887, "were mere machine tenders. Such a life is not life. One respects a man for hating such work." Few could avoid the physical risks inherent in their jobs, and many lost their limbs or their sight in industrial accidents. Most earned less than two dollars a day while working twelve hours a day, six days a week. Those who prospered most, the "iron elite," were the owners, but they did not feel a social responsibility for the plight of their workers. Those associated with the industrial magnates — the bankers and lawyers — also enjoyed Pittsburgh's prosperity without bearing the burden of a social conscience.

For a while, industrial unions were effective in ameliorating conditions for unskilled workers, but as the end of the nineteenth century approached, managers had regained the upper hand, breaking strikes by using scabs, in particular black workers from the South who had otherwise been excluded from better-paying jobs. Andrew Carnegie's triumph in the Homestead strike of 1892 freed the managerial class from countervailing organized worker power.

By the turn of the century, Carnegie had moved to New York City, deserting the town that had made him wealthy; he retired in 1901 to devote his time to philanthropy and his fortune to the building of libraries. (Perhaps his fixation on libraries was based on the fact that as a youth he was barred from using the Pittsburgh Mechanics' and Apprentices' Library.) His motto was "The man who dies rich dies disgraced." Apparently, he felt no disgrace from the dreadful working conditions he had provided his employees.

A Distinctive Social Landscape

The first permanent European settlers in Pittsburgh were English and Scottish, but by the mid-nineteenth century they were joined by the Irish escaping the potato famine and the Germans avoiding military conscription. There was ample cheap farmland available, and unskilled labor was needed in manufacturing. The earlier craft system had given way to a production method that capitalized on the unskilled labor of the abundant immigrant population. The Catholic Irish in Pittsburgh were subject to the same exclusionary practices their brethren had received in Boston, but the Protestant Germans generally had skills or capital to buy land. By 1860, foreign-born residents made up half of Pittsburgh's population, and by 1880 seven of ten were of foreign parentage.

Pittsburgh also experienced the second wave of immigration from southern and eastern Europe in the 1890s. Pittsburgh's engines of steel needed more cheap, unskilled labor. Italians, Poles, Hungarians, Slovenians, Ukrainians, and other eastern Europeans were drawn to these industrial jobs in the Smoky City. A substantial number of African Americans, leaving sharecropping to find work, migrated north, but discrimination followed them from the South. Many among the second-wave immigrants came to Pittsburgh because they knew people there who had migrated earlier. Others came because they had heard about the abundant industrial opportunities for unskilled laborers.

Wedged among the factories and mills were housing, markets, schools, and churches for Pittsburgh's new residents. Ethnic neighborhoods with their transplanted cultures grew around the industrial factories. Each had its own newspaper in its native language and businesses that would supply familiar foods and goods. The Irish first settled in Pittsburgh on the south side and in an area known as the Point near the rivers. German neighborhoods spread across the river to Allegheny, then a separate city, but later incorporated into the City of Pittsburgh. The Poles first settled in Pittsburgh's Strip District along the bank of the Allegheny River in houses earlier inhabited by Germans and Irish. Later they moved to homes on Herron Hill, known generally as "Polish Hill." By 1903, Pittsburgh's population had swelled to over 385,000, an increase of almost 50 percent in a single decade. One-third of the population had emigrated from Italy and Poland.

By 1900, it was apparent that the new immigrants were not "birds of passage" intent on returning home, but rather settlers who had made Pittsburgh their permanent home. They built religious structures and sectarian schools, and they formed fraternal organizations that structured their communities. For example, Poles living in the Strip built a $100,000 Romanesque church, a $70,000 parish house, and a $41,000 parochial school.

German, Irish, and English immigrants who had arrived decades earlier had moved out of crowded ethnic neighborhoods into streetcar suburbs, living close to the network of public transportation that would take them to work each day. When they could accumulate the capital to purchase a home — between $500 and $1,500 for the down payment — Italians and Poles would join the exodus out of the center city.

The unfettered economy of Pittsburgh made a few entrepreneurs very rich, but unlike the Brahmins of Boston, most of the wealthy iron elite did not abandon work to follow intellectual or public service pursuits. Their contributions to the city were measured in capital accumulated and tonnage produced, not in culture. As compared to that of Boston, aesthetic growth in Pittsburgh was modest. The entrepreneurs' sons, however, would be sent east for college at Yale or Princeton.

Pittsburgh was a working-class town driven by business interests and profit. The elite would hunt and fish, but they would not establish museums or opera companies as the Brahmins had in Boston. The entertainment that was available was aimed at a working-class audience. Amusement parks flourished. As the *Pittsburg Survey* of 1907 reported: "A girl who cuts onions for $.75 a day cares very little for the polished piano."

Pittsburgh and Baseball

As one of America's largest western cities in the nineteenth century, Pittsburgh had long provided a venue for sports. Horse racing, boxing, wrestling, cockfighting, and bowling flourished, and all presented opportunities for gambling. Professional baseball became the premier commercial spectator sport, an affordable diversion for the working class. A Pittsburgh club had been a charter member of the American Association in 1882, and that club jumped to the National League in 1887. Nicknamed "the Innocents," the Pittsburgh club never captured a championship. It would take Barney Dreyfuss's ownership, leadership, and resources to turn the Pittsburgh club—now called the Pirates—into champions. Dreyfuss would operate the franchise for thirty-two years, and his team would finish in the first division in twenty-six of those seasons.

Veterans returning from the Civil War first brought the game of baseball to the Smoky City. Amateur teams representing neighborhoods and workplaces played games throughout the city. They often drew enormous crowds and daily mention in the press. One restriction on play remained immutable: no games were played on Sunday in a town with blue laws where strict Sabbatarianism prevailed.

The Fourth Game

After two days of delay for travel and bad weather, the rain finally stopped. Pirates club secretary W. H. Locke consulted the weather forecaster, who advised that "there will be a clear spot in the sky this afternoon." The fourth game of the Series would be held on Tuesday, October 6, 1903.

This is what the Pittsburgh faithful awaited. As Ralph S. Davis wrote for the *Pittsburgh Press,* "Reading accounts of far-away ball games in the newspapers is not what the fans crave. They want to see the players in the flesh performing. They want to join in the shouts over some clever bit of work, and applaud the home team when it wins."

The wooden hulk of Exposition Park in Allegheny, across the river from Pittsburgh, had hosted Pirates games since 1891. The park, like the Huntington Avenue Grounds, had a vast playing field—400 feet down each foul line and 450 in center field. These dimensions were typical in the dead-ball era, when a league's leader would count his home runs in the single digits, and those mostly of the inside-the-park variety.

In 1875, the Allegheny Exposition had been held along the flats on the north shore of the Allegheny River. In addition to promoting the manufacturing muscle of the western metropolis, the exposition offered horse racing, circuses, and concerts. In 1882, the American Association Alleghenies played their baseball games on the exposition grounds, but the area was subject to periodic flooding. The Pittsburgh entry in the 1890

Players League built a grandstand for Exposition Park, and the Pirates occupied that structure in 1891. The flooding continued, however. For example, the Allegheny River overflowed its banks on July 4, 1902, before a scheduled doubleheader between Pittsburgh and Brooklyn. More than a foot of water covered large parts of the outfield. It was agreed that all hits into the water would be considered ground-rule singles. The Pirates swept the doubleheader.

Although the rain had ceased by Tuesday morning, an overcast that "hung ominously" would hold the crowd down to 7,600 for the fourth game. The sun needed to dry out the infield did not make an appearance: "That orb persistently refused to show its face except in a most desultory manner," wrote a *Boston Herald* reporter. Despite the best efforts of "Groundskeeper Murphy," as he was referred to in the press, the outfield was in "frightful shape" and the infield was slippery. Dreyfuss had the grounds crew sprinkle sand and sawdust on the field, but playing conditions were even more treacherous than usual.

At the Monongahela House, the Boston team and its loyal Rooters climbed into fifteen open carriages and two busses for the crosstown trip to Exhibition Park. Led by Professor Karl Frederick William Guenther's Italian band at a "double quick time," the parade included the uniformed players and their Royal Rooters. It was, the *Boston Post* reported, an "imposing cavalcade."

Umpire Hank O'Day called for the first pitch at 2:56, a few minutes early. The afternoon contest featured the return to the mound of the first- and third-game Pirates winner, Charles Louis "Deacon" Phillippe. It would prove to be another heartbreaking game for the Boston nine. Phillippe would tower over his Boston opponents through the first eight innings and then escape with a 5–4 victory. Bill Dineen, who had captured Boston's only victory in the second game of the Series, was shaky from the start, giving up three singles and one run in the first inning. Boston could manage but one single through the first four innings, then scratched in a tally in the fifth on two hits. The Pirates matched that with one of their own in the bottom of the fifth frame on Ginger Beaumont's center-field triple followed by

Leach's single to right. The Pirates added three runs in the seventh when Leach's triple scored two runs, followed by Wagner's single that plated Leach with, as it turned out, the eventual winning run.

The Pirates would need every one of their runs, because the Americans scored three in the top of the ninth on five singles. According to the *Pittsburgh Dispatch,* the "dratted Boston [club] waked to the fact that they could play ball." The rally transformed Boston's somnolent Royal Rooters into "howling maniacs, overjoyed to a delirious stage." As their heroes mounted the comeback, "the Boston rooters had simply lost control of themselves, war dances, cheers, yells and songs resounding clear across the Allegheny River." The *Dispatch* characterized the Royal Rooters as "the feature of the game." Their bold effort notwithstanding, the Americans fell short when little-used substitute Jack O'Brien, batting for Dineen, popped up to end the contest. "Another finale like that," the *Dispatch* opined, "and there will be a wholesale canceling of life insurance policies in Pittsburgh." The adoring Pittsburgh crowd carried Phillippe off the field on their shoulders.

GAME 4

Team	1	2	3	4	5	6	7	8	9	R	H	E
Boston	0	0	0	0	1	0	0	0	3	4	9	1
Pittsburgh	1	0	0	0	1	0	3	0	x	5	12	1

Some observers thought the Boston squad had become "easy meat" for the Pittsburgh nine, although neither team had played well that day. Now ahead three games to one, it was only a matter of time (and two further victories for Pittsburgh) until the team from the west wore the crown as champions. The betting odds had now turned to 10–7 in favor of Pittsburgh. Many of the Pirates' loyal followers concluded that Boston was simply not in their class. But the *Boston Globe* reminded Boston followers that "the Collins tribe are gritty," and the *Pittsburgh Dispatch* cautioned its readers:

> The gang filed out of the park last evening pretty well satisfied that the only time when it is a cinch that Boston's beat is when

> the other team is 1,000,000 runs ahead and such people as Collins, Doherty, Stahl, Freeman, Dineen, Young, Criger and some others are locked up. Even then they are liable to turn in with the subs and do a whole lot of damage.

Despite the dimming prospects for the Boston club in the Series, as promised at eight that evening the Royal Rooters' Italian band entertained an overflow crowd of five thousand at the Monongahela House "with a varied and appreciated concert" lasting three hours. The local press was impressed with the fairness and good spirit of the Boston fanatics: "It was the fairest crowd of visiting rooters ever gathered at Exposition Park, and the local people enjoyed their presence," reported the *Pittsburgh Press*. To change their luck, however, the Rooters discharged the Italian band and engaged a German band for game five and an Irish band for game six. Everyone hoped the prediction of Pittsburgh's weather clerk for more rain would be wrong.

The Fifth Game

A large crowd of 12,322 turned out on October 7 in perfect weather to witness the fifth game of the World Series, the second contest held at Pittsburgh's Exposition Park. The crowd was five or six deep on the playing field, secured behind ropes. Others roosted on nearby hillsides and rooftops. The *Boston Herald* reported: "It was a great day for a game of ball and the fans turned out in fine fashion to see the sport." They had come to see their Pirates continue what appeared to be their inevitable march to victory, having won three of the first four contests. Two more victories and the first World Series between the National and American Leagues was theirs. The "bright skies" this day, however, would favor Boston.

Boston's Royal Rooters turned out in large numbers as well. None had deserted the cause. The German band the Bostonians had hired for this fifth game of the Series led the march from the Monongahela House and continuously puffed "popular airs" on their horns for nine innings. The

Rooters, decked out in red badges, carrying red, white, and blue canes and parasols, marched into the park in lines of four. Throughout the contest, Mike McGreevey sang Irish tunes and danced on top of the Boston players' bench. The wife of Hobe Ferris, Boston's second baseman, yelled inspiration from her seat that could be heard throughout the park. A delegation of Patsy Dougherty's old friends cheered Boston's left fielder, who had played ball in nearby Homestead. A train from Cleveland carried fans of Cy Young to watch the old master pitch.

As a precaution, Pittsburgh owner Barney Dreyfuss had ordered supporting beams erected under Section J, lest the Royal Rooters' "frenzied enthusiasm" break down the park's grandstand. The Pittsburgh crowd looked on in awe, enjoying "the half-crazy antics of the Boston rooters," but soon joined in chants and cheers of their own, at least until it was clear the game had gone to the visitors from the Hub. Even the Pirates great hurler Deacon Phillippe could not pitch two days in a row without a rest. Instead, manager Fred Clarke went with Brickyard Kennedy, a controversial choice.

The portents favored Kennedy. He hailed from Bellaire, Ohio, sixty miles to the southwest on the Ohio River, and many hometowners had traveled to Pittsburgh to watch him pitch. It was also Kennedy's thirty-sixth birthday. He was eager to twirl, and he placed a wager that he would win his game.

With the Pirates holding a commanding three games to one lead, a fourth loss for the Boston squad with two more contests scheduled for Pittsburgh would certainly have made the uphill climb too steep to scale. With a Boston victory in game five, however, the World Series would tighten and the prospects for the Americans improve markedly.

The day started well for Kennedy and the Pirates. He dodged a bullet in the first inning when Jimmy Collins's triple went for naught; he was thrown out at home by Honus Wagner on a ground ball. A walk by Freeman and an infield hit by Parent loaded the bases, but Lachance spoiled the rally by popping out to third.

It was Cy Young's turn again on the mound for the Americans. He had lost game one in Boston the prior week and relieved for seven innings in the third game, another Boston defeat. This day, however, Young would be very much in control, and "Clarke's crew went to pieces," reported the *Pittsburgh Gazette.*

The sixth inning of the fifth game proved to be the turning point of the 1903 World Series. Kennedy had held the Americans scoreless through five innings, "mixing up his speed and benders with great success," observed the *Pittsburgh Gazette.* Likewise, Young kept the Pirates off the board. Although it was a scoreless pitchers' duel, rooters for both sides had much to cheer about, as both clubs exhibited flawless fielding.

The Boston offense finally exploded in the sixth frame. The first three Boston batters reached base thanks to careless play by Pittsburgh, including a dropped ball by Wagner that could have forced a runner at third. With the bases loaded Kennedy walked Lachance, forcing in Boston's first run. Wagner then threw wildly on a ground ball, and another run scored. ("Even the king of ballplayers is fallible," the *Pittsburgh Press* reminded its readers.) Catcher Criger bunted home still another run. Shaken, Kennedy grooved two pitches: Cy Young responded with a triple into the crowd in left field, driving home two additional runs; Dougherty followed with a triple of his own. Two triples, a collection of singles and some sloppy fielding by the Pirates' infielders resulted in six unearned runs, and the complexion of the Series had changed. The Royal Rooters' German band played "There Will Be a Hot Time in the Old Town Tonight."

Boston added four more runs in the seventh with another triple by Dougherty, his second in two innings. Still another triple by Stahl led to the final Boston tally in the eighth. No Pirate progressed beyond second base until the bottom half of the eighth inning, and the National League team was on the verge of being whitewashed in game five. With the game well beyond reach at 11–0, most of the Pirates fans had deserted the stadium. Young then gave up a triple to Leach with two men on base that scored Pittsburgh's two runs and avoided the "ignominy of a shutout." Young allowed only six hits and no walks, while pitching his customary complete game. As the *Boston Herald* headline read the next day, "Cy Young Twirls the Sphere in Gilt-Edge Style."

GAME 5

Team	1	2	3	4	5	6	7	8	9	R	H	E
Boston	0	0	0	0	0	6	4	1	0	11	14	2
Pittsburgh	0	0	0	0	0	0	0	2	0	2	6	4

The game took exactly two hours to complete, and the Boston Americans had regained their equilibrium. The *Pittsburgh Press* concluded: "It was a bitter blow to the followers of the Pirates, but the locals did not deserve to win, judging from the way they played." Honus Wagner was a particular disappointment with his multiple costly errors and a hitless performance. The *Pittsburgh Gazette* wrote: "It was Wagner who must bear the brunt of the defeat. But as Hans does not do tricks of that kind often, the cranks can afford to forgive him." The long season had worn down even as great a ballplayer as Wagner. It was a sad birthday for Kennedy. It would be his last appearance on the mound after twelve years in the National League.

This was very much Cy Young's game. "My, how he did put them over!" gushed the *Boston Herald*. Here, finally, said the *Pittsburgh Gazette*, was the masterful "Grand Old Man of Baseball," "the real thing," staving off three potential scoring chances by the Pirates in the first five innings while leading the Boston nine to a much-needed victory.

Cy Young

In 1901, Ban Johnson had awarded Charles Somers the exclusive American League right to sign baseball's leading pitcher, Cy Young, then under contract with the St. Louis Perfectos of the National League. At thirty-four, Young was approaching what for most ballplayers would have been the end of their baseball career. In fact, Young was only halfway through his twenty-two-year career.

When Charles Somers offered Young a sizable increase in salary to $3,500 a year and a three-year contract, something the St. Louis club was unwilling to do, Young made the move. Young's St. Louis catcher, Lou Criger, had already accepted an offer to join the Boston club. Young's wife,

Robba, who had wilted in the St. Louis summer heat, was delighted to make the move to the East Coast.

In an era when professional baseball players showed more athletic skill than moral rectitude, Young genuinely represented all-American virtues. Born and raised on a farm in Tuscarawas County in central Ohio with only a limited formal education and few business skills, Young became a national symbol of uncorrupted virtue. Young's public persona as the honest farmer, the man of the land endowed with country values, was not a public relations ploy. This was an accurate portrayal of a man of the land who was a devout Sabbatarian. He insisted that his baseball contract allow him to decline pitching assignments on Sunday. In a professional game often played by ruffians, gamblers, and alcoholics, Cy Young stood out as the embodiment of bucolic virtue.

Young used to explain that he had gained his nickname "Cyclone" in 1890 while playing for the Canton, Ohio, baseball club of the Tri-State League. Young recalled that when his pitches splintered some boards of Canton's Pastime Park fence, one of the fellows said the stands "looked like a cyclone struck it." Within two years the moniker "Cyclone" was shortened to the now familiar "Cy," leaving his given name of Denton True Young for trivia buffs. There may be alternative explanations for his nickname. Many ballplayers with rural backgrounds were called "Cyrus," and Young certainly fit that description. In addition, the big Ohio boy's pitching featured a "cyclone," another name for a fastball at the time.

Before joining the Boston Americans, Young had enjoyed an exemplary nine-year career pitching for the Cleveland Nationals, referred to by the locals as the "Spiders." Throughout the 1890s his legend grew along with his accomplishments. Young consistently demonstrated magnificent control of his pitches. He was a large man in an era when most ballplayers were of slight build. Six feet, two inches tall and weighing 210 pounds, he towered over the opposition.

In 1893, the National League moved the pitcher's box five feet farther from home plate to its current sixty feet, six inches. Most pitchers failed to make a successful transition to the new distance. Young, on the other hand, continued his supremacy over National League hitters. By 1895, he was among baseball's premier hurlers, combining a fastball and curve with a slow ball (change of pace) and pinpoint control, regularly leading the league in fewest walks per game.

In 1899, Cleveland owner Frank Robison, despairing at the state of his baseball business in Cleveland, purchased a second National League franchise in St. Louis, which he renamed the Perfectos, and moved his best players to his new club, including star pitcher Cy Young. After the 1900 season, Robison deeply hurt Young's feelings when he wrongly accused his star hurler of malingering, a charge unsupported by the facts of his performance for the Perfectos. Robison's actions were shortsighted. Young eagerly accepted Charles Somers's generous offer to join the American League and would anchor the Boston's pitching staff for eight seasons. He then played for Cleveland before finishing his illustrious career with a brief stint on the Boston National League club.

Young's accomplishments during his full major league career are rightly celebrated. His 511 victories, 750 complete games, and 7,356 innings pitched are records unlikely ever to be bested. On October 4, 1890, in his first season in the majors, he pitched and won both games of a doubleheader. For fourteen consecutive seasons starting in 1891, he won twenty or more games a year. He won thirty or more games in five of those seasons. During a four-game span in 1904, Young pitched twenty-three consecutive scoreless innings. And on May 4, 1904, he pitched the third perfect game in major league history.

With Boston's resounding victory in game five, thanks to Cy Young's twirling and some timely hitting, the embers of hope remained alive for the Boston squad. Perhaps they had "struck their gait." As they had after their games in Boston, that night both clubs enjoyed the local entertainment. At the invitation of theater manager Harry Davis, the players took in *Notre Dame,* which opened that week at the rebuilt Grand Opera House after a long run at New York City's Daly Theatre. The *Pittsburgh Press* described it as a "tremendous scenic spectacle" adapting Victor Hugo's story of the love-struck hunchback in the cathedral. The appearance of the champion baseball players was as much an attraction to the attendees as the performance. In fact, the band played a special rendition of "See the Conquering Hero Comes" as a tribute to the players of both clubs as they entered the theater. After the performance, the players were introduced to members of the company, including Eva Taylor, formerly of the Castle Square stock company of Boston, and Charles Abbe of the Boston Museum.

HONUS WAGNER

Honus Wagner, the good-natured and modest "Flying Dutchman," was a native son of Pittsburgh who escaped the coal mines to excel on the baseball diamond. He retired in 1917 with a career batting average of .327; his Hall of Fame plaque proclaims that Wagner had "scored more runs, made more hits and stole more bases than any other player in the history of his league." Some say he was the greatest baseball player ever.

6

The Hometown Favorite: Honus Wagner

By the sixth game of the 1903 World Series, the Pittsburgh club had learned that the Boston nine would not be an easy mark. Having lost three of the first four games, the Americans might have simply folded with the next three games scheduled for western Pennsylvania. Yet Collins's boys fought back valiantly to close the match to three games to two. If Boston could win the sixth contest, it would even the Series, ensure a return trip east to Boston for the eighth and maybe ninth games, and shift the momentum toward the Boston club.

Perhaps the Royal Rooters' persistent chanting and ranting were making a difference? McGreevey's men did not make the trip all the way to Pittsburgh to see their heroes lose meekly. After all, these American League ballplayers had pluck. These young men had not been afraid to take the risk of jumping to an outlawed, rival circuit where they would be blackballed from any future play in the National League. Now that peace had come, it was time to determine which circuit would reign supreme on the diamond.

The Pirates players were resolved to take the edge in the match by winning the sixth game on their home turf. The antics of Boston's Royal Rooters had energized the Pittsburgh faithful to equal their noise and enthusiasm.

The Pirates were a proud club, the winner of three consecutive league pennants. If they were to prevail, however, their stalwart shortstop, Honus Wagner, would have to break out of his hitting slump and lead them to victory as he had so many times in the past.

The Coal Miner's Son

Out of the Pennsylvania coal mines and into the hearts of baseball fans, Johannes Peter Wagner was a genuine original. Wagner was a barrel-chested, powerful bull of a man, with massive shoulders, long arms, huge hands, and bowed legs. (It was said that his legs were so bowed that he "couldn't catch a pig in an alley.") The *Louisville Commercial* once wrote of Wagner that at five-feet-eleven and two hundred pounds he "is a splendidly built man cut on a generous pattern. In fact his whole build is very much after the order of a one-story brick house." His plain face was etched as if out of concrete, and it surrounded a most conspicuous nose. Barney Dreyfuss described him as "the most modest gentleman I have ever had the pleasure of knowing." A reserved and simple man, Wagner was the hometown favorite and a hero to his Pittsburgh fans.

Wagner loved to hunt and fish, his two off-season diversions. A man of simple tastes, he loved ham and eggs and especially pies. A writer for the *Pittsburgh Gazette* once remarked that "Honus eats more pie than the law allows." He never abandoned his working-class, stoic roots. His skill at the national game — Branch Rickey called him "the greatest player of all time" — was an immigrant success story and an inspiration for millions of young boys. At the turn of the twentieth century, almost half of all Americans were immigrants or the children of immigrants. Wagner was a splendid role model for all these new Americans.

Wagner's parents, Peter and Katheryn Wagner, had arrived in Pittsburgh from Prussia. They had married in 1864 in Dirmingen in the Saar region of western Germany. Peter's family had lived in Dirmingen for generations working as farmers or, like Peter, in the coal mines. He was drawn to America to improve the economic condition of what he hoped would be a large family. He also knew that the Prussian kaiser's military adventures posed the threat of conscription. Pittsburgh was known throughout Prussia as "The Forge of the Universe," with plenty of work available in the mines, mills, and factories. In 1867, Peter left his new wife with his family in Germany, but within a year she joined him in western Pennsylvania.

The family settled in Chartiers, a coal mining town four miles from downtown Pittsburgh, but there was no reason for the new residents to travel to the Smoky City. All the family's needs could be met in Chartiers or its twin village on the other side of the creek, Mansfield. In 1894, the two towns would merge and rename themselves in honor of the region's leading citizen, Scottish immigrant Andrew Carnegie.

Katheryn gave birth to nine children, but only six survived infancy. Johannes Peter Wagner was the fourth surviving son. Born February 24, 1874, the youngster was called "Hans" or "Hannes" — short for Johannes — by his family. Peter Wagner encouraged his sons to engage in athletics. He would lead them on jogs through the village and then in calisthenics.

The Wagners spoke only German at their modest home at 119 Railroad Avenue, near the fourteen tracks that ran along Chartiers Creek to the nearby rail yard. Devout Lutherans, the family attended services at St. Johannis Evangelisch Lutherische Kirche, where the ceremony was conducted in German. Chartiers was filled with German immigrants. Although raised in a German language environment, the Wagner children spoke English without an accent.

Peter Wagner provided for his family by mining coal. The arduous work, digging coal out of a hillside with pick axes, suited the strong father. After six years of schooling, twelve-year-old Honus joined his father in the coal fields. Young boys were employed to work as "breaker boys," separating the coal from the rock. Child labor laws allowed boys to work in the mines at age twelve and in the factories at age thirteen, so the following year, Honus worked part-time in a steel mill and helped out his older brother Charley, who had become a barber. When the family's finances allowed, Wagner returned to school and completed all his formal education by age fifteen.

Baseball was an important part of immigrant life, and the boys of Carnegie played whenever possible, with lunchtime contests and games illuminated by gas lamps at dusk. Boys played on community, church, and company teams. Eventually, three boys from small Carnegie, Pennsylvania, would make it to the major leagues—the two Wagner brothers, Al and Honus, and their friend Patsy Flaherty.

Honus's older brother Al was the first to leave town to pursue a baseball career. He was the star player of the family in the minor leagues, paving the path for his younger brother Honus. He counseled Honus to learn every position, increasing his chances to be picked up by a club in need. Soon Honus was playing regularly for local semiprofessional clubs. When they were not playing baseball, the two Wagner brothers would hang around the pool hall in Chartiers.

Honus Wagner first played baseball for pay in 1895 at age twenty-one, certainly a late start for someone destined for major league greatness. Al Wagner, who was playing third base for the Steubenville, Ohio, club, told the owner, George Moreland, that his brother "was a peach." Honus joined the squad for $35 a month, from which he paid for his own uniform and shoes. The minor league game was particularly unstable at the time: Wagner played that season for five different teams in three leagues in three states.

The following season, Wagner played for the Paterson, New Jersey, Silk Citys in the Atlantic League at $125 a month, earning more that summer than the average worker earned in an entire year. Ed Barrow, the future general manager of the New York Yankees (as well as manager of the 1918 Red Sox), owned the Paterson club, and he is generally credited with having discovered Wagner's baseball talent. Wagner enjoyed his time in New Jersey, joining a club that featured four future major leaguers. Paterson was a prosperous city of one hundred thousand, seventeen miles west of New York City and home to one hundred silk mills, making the immigrant metropolis the largest silk-producing city in the world.

Wagner was well regarded by the local newspapers for his attitude, skills, and work habits, although he chewed tobacco and smoked cigars, as did many of his fellow ballplayers. The local German population, numbering more than ten thousand, adopted Wagner, "the German war horse," as its hero. He was a remarkably versatile player, playing all positions that year except catcher. He started the season at first base, pitched some innings, and ended the season at third.

Although he began the 1897 season in the minors as Paterson's clean-up hitter, by midyear Wagner was the subject of much interest by major league scouts who regularly came to the New York area. Claude McFarlan, an outfielder with the new Atlantic League franchise in Norfolk, wrote to his friend Harry Pulliam, president of the Louisville Colonels of the National League, touting Wagner. Eight collect telegrams later, Pulliam agreed to cross the Hudson to see the young ballplayer. Pulliam, who would be associated with Wagner and the Pirates for years to come, cabled McFarlan:

> Saw your miracle play today. Don't bother me anymore about him. Whatever gave you the idea that anybody with such gates-ajar legs can play baseball? I'm sending this collect, darn your hide. Let it be a lesson to you.

Pulliam did not leave town, however, and within a few days realized his initial impression was wrong. After hard bargaining with the owner of the Paterson club, the Colonels acquired the rights to sign Wagner to a major league contract.

In sixty-one games with Louisville that season, Wagner showed enormous promise, batting .336. His salary was doubled to $250 a month, and Wagner was now certain that playing ball was preferable to working in a coal mine. After the season, Honus and his brother Al (sometimes referred to in the newspapers as "Butts" Wagner) returned to Carnegie, where they jointly bought a poolroom. The following year, brother Al had his one stint in the majors with Washington of the National League, while Honus's career was just beginning.

The National League folded the Louisville Colonels franchise after the 1899 season. Colonels owner Barney Dreyfuss bought an interest in the Pittsburgh club and announced on December 9, 1899, that the hometown hero, Honus Wagner, would now play for Pittsburgh. (His salary was increased to $2,100 for the season.) Fellow Carnegie boyhood chum Patsy Flaherty also signed with the Pirates, although he would play only four games for the club that year and bounce around the league during the remainder of his nine-year major league career. Wagner, on the other hand, would spend the remainder of his stellar twenty-one-year career with the Pirates.

The bow-legged, barrel-chested son of a coal miner with hands like meat hooks would accumulate a .327 lifetime average in the major league and repeatedly lead the league in batting average, singles, doubles, triples, and stolen bases. Until 1903, Wagner would play wherever Pirates manager Fred Clarke needed him—generally half the time in the outfield, the other half in the infield. He even pitched on two occasions. From 1903 until 1917, however, Wagner settled in the infield spot that would make him one of the game's all-time greats—shortstop. Boston's *Daily News* called Wagner the "Hercules of the diamond."

The Way the Game Was Played

Although baseball at the turn of the twentieth century would be quite familiar to those who follow today's pennant races, there were some notable differences in the sport Honus Wagner mastered. First of all, today's manicured fields would have been unheard of in 1903. A ball field was an open spot of ground surrounded on three sides by wooden grandstands. The grass—where there was grass—was not tended as it is today. The infield was strewn with rocks and pebbles. (They say of Wagner's fielding prowess that he would scoop up a ground ball with whatever detritus lay in its path and toss the amalgam toward first base. The first object to arrive was probably the baseball.)

There were no dugouts on the field until 1909. Players sat in an enclosed bench on the field between the grandstand and the foul line. The National League adopted the seventeen-inch-wide pentagonal home plate in 1900 and the American in 1903. Home plate had started as a round disk, then was replaced with a twelve-inch diamond in 1869. The new pentagonal plate was designed to assist the umpires in calling strikes, and it gave an edge to the pitchers. Despite the large strike zone, umpires still got the calls wrong, according to observers who were always unhappy with their decisions.

By 1903, all players wore gloves, but they were more like today's batting gloves, designed for protection rather than assistance in fielding. Until 1953, players would leave their gloves on the field when their team came to bat. Catchers wore masks and chest protectors but no shin guards until 1908, when Roger Bresnahan of the New York Giants introduced the protection. Of course, no batting helmets were worn. (They did not become mandatory until 1971.) Ballparks rarely had locker facilities for members of visiting teams, who would dress at their hotel and ride to the park in an open horse-drawn carriage referred to as a "tally-ho."

If they could, players played while injured; their contracts were not guaranteed, and a player who could not play was not paid. Uniforms were made of heavy wool, but no numbers would appear on the backs until 1929, when first adopted by the Yankees and the Indians. Uniforms were washed irregularly. (The Chicago club that threw the 1919 World Series had first called themselves the "Black Sox" because owner Charles Comiskey never laundered their uniforms.)

At the turn of the century, a new baseball was intended to last a whole contest, and it was retrieved from the stands after a foul hit. (Teams even stationed guards outside the fences to retrieve any balls hit outside the enclosure.) In general, teams would use three or four balls a game. The 1916 Cubs were the first team to allow fans to keep the balls hit into the stands. (Cubs fans at some later date developed the custom of throwing back into the field of play any home runs hit by opponent players.) Baseballs at the turn of the century turned soft from the beating they took as the game progressed. Infielders never knew how they would bounce, especially on a rough infield. Pitchers would also add a variety of foreign substances to the spheres to enhance their erratic flight toward home base. After a few innings, the ball had turned dark, moist, and soft.

By the turn of the century, pitchers hurled from the "pitcher's plate" (now called the rubber), twenty-four inches long and six inches wide, set, as it is today, at sixty feet, six inches from home plate. Pitching overhand was not allowed until 1885. Earlier, the pitcher had tossed the ball underhand from a rectangular box five and a half feet long and four feet wide, whose forward line was only forty-five feet from home plate. In 1893, the distance was lengthened from the pitcher's "box" to home — the terminology remained even though the actual box had long disappeared — but now pitchers could stride forward off an elevated mound. (Even today, a pitcher replaced after a poor performance is said to have been "knocked out of the box.") In 1903, the mound height was standardized at fifteen inches above the field, although over the century that height would be changed to encourage more scoring (lower the mound) or decrease scoring (raise the mound).

At the turn of the century, it was expected that a major league pitcher would throw complete games. During the 1901–1904 period, pitchers completed 85 percent of their games. (On June 25, 1903, Wiley Piatt of the Boston Beaneaters pitched two complete games in one day against the Pirates. He lost them both.) Pitchers would hurl a variety of offerings: fastballs, incurves, outcurves, reverse curves, inshoots, downshoots, jump balls, rising balls, and drops. Pitchers would brush batters off the plate with high inside fastballs. Games generally took about two hours or less to complete, with no breaks (as we have today for television commercials) and few calls for relief pitchers.

Until 1877, the home team batted first. In 1878, the two team captains flipped a coin to decide which squad would bat first. It was an advantage to bat first, because the ball was fresh and hittable. Even as late as the 1890s, there were some instances when the home team batted first, but by 1903 today's practice had become standard. The visitor took first at bat.

Starting in 1901 in the National League and 1903 in the American League, a batter was charged a strike for each of his first two foul hits. Previously, foul hits were not counted as strikes at all, which explains in part the higher batting averages of the premodern period. The number of called balls for a walk was not standardized at four until 1889. (In fact, balls and strikes were not called at all until 1863.)

The bats used in 1903 were heavy by comparison to those used today. Until 1893, a bat could be flat on one side, like a cricket bat, making it easier to execute the bunt, or "baby hits" as they were called then. A batter who made good contact with the soft baseball might be pleased to drive it three hundred feet, generally far short of the outfield wall. As a result, outfielders played extremely shallow and often threw runners out at first on ground balls through the infield. Ground rules varied in each stadium, but normally a ball that bounded into the stands fair on a bounce was considered a home run. (Chances were good in any case that a ball hit that far could not be retrieved before a runner had circumnavigated the bases.) There were no nonplayer baseball coaches for the offensive team until 1907, when the Giants' John McGraw hired a former player to perform that role. Until then, two players not due up at bat that inning manned the baselines as coaches.

The small squads, numbering perhaps fourteen players, included five pitchers. Every position player played every game. The game featured "inside baseball," singles, bunts, sacrifices, hit-and-runs, and steals. Batters would choke up on their bats to punch the ball through the infield for a single or a double. The out-of-the-park home run was a rare exception and not a core feature of the entertainment.

Games typically began in the middle of the afternoon, normally 3:00 P.M. or later, so that fans could attend after their day's work. An announcer with a megaphone would call out to the stands who was at bat. Longer contests in spring or fall might have to be called because of darkness. (There were no lights for night games.)

Umpired by a single arbiter, players took advantage of the fact the umpire had but two eyes. They bent the rules whenever possible and heaped scorn upon the ump when his calls disadvantaged their team. The umpire would stand behind the catcher until a man got on base. Then he would move out behind the pitcher to call balls and strikes. Until 1909, umpires did not signal strikes or outs. It was left to the spectators to figure out what was going on in the game, unencumbered at that time by electronic scoreboards or public address announcers. The hand-operated scoreboard showed the inning scores and the totals of runs but did not indicate hits and errors as they do today. The newspaper sports pages—a relatively new media phenomenon at the turn of the century—printed the box scores each day.

In general, baseball games were banned on Sundays under local blue laws. Sunday games were legal only in Detroit, St. Louis, Chicago, and Cincinnati. Brooklyn once tried to circumvent the blue laws by not charging admission for its Sunday home games while requiring all attendees to purchase an expensive scorecard to enter the grandstand. The ploy did not work; the players were arrested, and Sunday baseball remained illegal.

Game Six

With one day's rest between starts, Bill Dineen took the mound for Boston on October 8 for the sixth game. This was his third start in the Series. He had won the second game in Boston and lost the fourth game earlier that week in Pittsburgh. The Pirates used the sore-armed "Goshen Schoolmaster," Sam Leever, giving Deacon Phillippe another day's rest. Leever was so sure he would win that he wagered $200 of his own money on the outcome. It would turn out to be a thrilling contest.

Leever started strong for the Pirates, facing the minimum six batters the first two innings. In the third frame, however, Boston scored three runs on singles by Collins and Stahl and an error by Pittsburgh third baseman Leach. The Boston Royal Rooters were out in numbers and made noise throughout the contest. The Pirates' own loyal followers, now self-proclaimed as the Champion Rooters, had given their Boston counterparts brightly colored umbrellas. The Boston crew, using tin horns to make a constant racket, ran up and down the aisles twirling their gag presents. And with the help of their hired band, they also began singing the popular song of the day, "Tessie."

Vaudevillian Jack Norworth wrote the lyrics to "Tessie." Norworth would have an even more fabulous hit in 1908 relating the story of Miss Katie Casey whose beau offered to take her out to a "theatre show." She replied "I'll tell you what you can do!"

> Take me out to the ball game.
> Take me out with the crowd.

Norworth, who had never seen a baseball game, had written the anthem for America's sport.

The Royal Rooters' "Tessie" songfest in Pittsburgh would take on mythical dimensions in Boston baseball history. While the Rooters sang, the Americans scored three runs in the third inning. Because the fanatics associated the song with Boston's rally, they continued the serenade throughout the contest. Led by Mike McGreevey, who danced a jig above Boston's bench and bellowed out the lyrics through his megaphone, the rooters sang the altered lyrics to "Tessie" they had devised the prior Monday when rain had postponed the fourth game. The singing further rallied the Boston troops and flustered their Pittsburgh opponents. They would sing to their hero, Jimmy Collins: "Jimmy, we love you dearly." The Pirates' Honus Wagner, on the other hand, was the particular object of their ridicule.

The lyrics for the "Tessie" song began "Tessie, you make me feel so badly." As adapted by the Royal Rooters to unsettle Wagner, the chorus ran:

> Honus, why do you hit so badly?
> Take a back seat and sit down.
> Honus, at bat you look so sadly,
> Hey, why don't you get out of town!

The rooters would then stomp their feet three times on the wooden bleachers, calling out "Bang! Bang! Bang!" and then one more time with emphasis chant, "Why don't you get out of town!" McGreevey explained to fellow rooter Jacob Morse that the singing would "charm the Pittsburgh players so that when they hear [the lyrics] their eye will lose its keenness and their arms their brawn. I believe in the power of music." They sang their song dozens of times. It seemed, said the *Pittsburgh Gazette,* "that Tessie was their mascot." At first, the Pittsburgh crowd welcomed the novelty of the Rooters' display, but eventually the cheers turned to jeers at its constant repetition as the Pirates' fortunes flagged.

Jimmy Collins paid tribute to the Royal Rooters after the contest: "I do not know what I would have done without them. Their aid in encouraging us to victory has meant lots and lots to us in these games. They share in the victory with us." Decades later, Honus Wagner would recall the Rooters' annoying refrain and admit that it disrupted his play during the first World Series.

Boston continued to add to its lead in game six. Errors by a distracted Wagner and Leach and a ground-rule triple by Stahl in the fifth inning counted two more Boston tallies. In the top of the seventh inning, Lachance followed Parent's triple with a double of his own, and Boston led 6–0. The game seemed safely in hand.

The Pirates' offense lay dormant until the team's turn in the seventh inning. As their loyalists boldly cheered, the Pirates quickly sliced the Boston lead in half, scoring three runs on three singles and a double by Clarke. The local crowd of more than eleven thousand fanatics became excited to the level of "almost drunken ecstasy." In its page one story, the *Boston Globe* reported that Pittsburgh fans, "roaring like the falls of Niagara," attempted to "disconcert" the visiting team by throwing confetti "to the breeze," covering Boston hurler Dineen with scraps of paper. With two out, Wagner and Beaumont walked, loading the bases. Claude Ritchey, the game's best "pinch" hitter (meaning, at that time, a batter who hit "in the pinch," rather than as a substitute for another player), came to bat. The *Boston Post* drew on a football analogy: "Picture Harvard having the ball on Yale's one-yard line on the third down at Soldiers Field." If Boston could stem this Pittsburgh tide, they would even the Series at three games apiece. Ritchey grounded to shortstop, forcing Bransfield at second.

The Americans had stopped the Pirates' rally in the seventh with a three-run lead intact, but Boston still had to face the combined forces of the

"Champions from the West" and a crowd thirsting for victory in the eighth and ninth frames. Boston manager Collins had relievers warming up, but Dineen pleaded to continue. Collins later commented that "little Willie [Dineen] was there with the goods." He retired the Pirates in order in the eighth, but the ninth inning would tell the tale.

Ginger Beaumont led off the final frame with a sharp single for Pittsburgh. The *Boston Post* reported: "Again the Boston rooters turned pale. Again Dineen clutched the ball with savage fury, and again the crowd of 11,000 now thoroughly mad people set up a howling." A Pittsburgh favorite, manager Fred Clarke, came up to bat. His vicious swing connected with the ball and Boston shortstop Parent dove for it, catching the orb "less than an inch off the ground." He shot the ball to first, completing the double play. Leach fouled out to the catcher to end the contest. It was a stirring victory for the American League champions.

GAME 6

Team	1	2	3	4	5	6	7	8	9	R	H	E
Boston	0	0	3	0	2	0	1	0	0	6	10	1
Pittsburgh	0	0	0	0	0	0	3	0	0	3	10	3

Dineen had collected the victory for Boston, his second of the Series, giving up three runs on ten hits. Sam Leever suffered his second loss for the Pirates, as the Americans scored six runs on ten hits. The Series was now tied at three games apiece. The clubs now knew that with only one remaining contest scheduled for Pittsburgh, there would have to be a return train trip to Boston for the conclusion of the Series. The nine-game tournament was down to the best-two-out-of-three games.

Barney Dreyfuss visited the clubhouse of the disheartened Pirates after the game, something he rarely did, in order to revitalize his troops and reinforce their confidence. After all, these Pirates were the great champions of the National League, the senior circuit! Unlike most other owners, Dreyfuss, the diminutive thirty-eight-year-old German-Jewish immigrant, was beloved by his players, and he returned their affection.

The Royal Rooters marched back to their hotel, waving their parasols and responding in good spirit to the badinage of the Pittsburgh onlookers. A carriage transported Mrs. Ferris, Mrs. Lachance, and Mrs. Young (the last of whom had arrived the day before from Ohio) back to the hotel.

The *Boston Post* reported that at 10:00 A.M. on Thursday, October 8, the day of the sixth game, Dreyfuss visited Jimmy Collins and Boston club management representatives at the Monongahela House. He requested that the scheduled seventh game be postponed from Friday until Saturday, when a larger crowd could be expected to attend. If the game was played on a Saturday, Pittsburgh's steelworks would grant the workers a half-day holiday. Westinghouse had offered to take one thousand tickets, but only if the game was played on Saturday. Although six thousand additional patrons could be expected, Collins absolutely refused the request. He knew that an extra day of rest would allow the Pirates' ace, Deacon Phillippe, to return to the box. As it turned out, however, Dreyfuss would not be deterred from his ploy. He would call off Friday's game anyway.

The Seventh Game

At noon on Friday, October 9, Pirates' manager Fred Clarke visited Exposition Park. He went through the motions of inspecting the field, the grandstands, and the boxes and reported his findings to Dreyfuss: "The wind over there must be sixty miles an hour. A player would run a great risk in playing in such weather." (The *Pittsburgh Gazette* concluded that Clarke must be "a pretty fair judge of wind storms, as he comes from Kansas.") Secretary W. H. Lodge of the Pittsburgh club even visited the weather bureau and was told by forecaster Ridgeway that the wind would blow steady that whole day, but that on Saturday it would be bright and fair. This, of course, was exactly what the Pittsburgh club wanted to hear.

Barney Dreyfuss then did what he had intended to do all along; he postponed the game scheduled for that afternoon because of "cold weather and high wind." The Boston Rooters were "disgusted" and Jimmy Collins was "dead sore." He told Clarke and Dreyfuss, "I think it's a shame." Admittedly, Friday was a chilly and blustery day in the Smoky City, more suitable for football than baseball, but the sun was out, the field was dry, and many games had been played under worse conditions. Boston fandom cried, "Cold weather! More like cold feet!"

Dreyfuss was perfectly within his rights in postponing the game. The agreement he had reached with Boston owner Henry Killilea establishing the Series gave the home team the right to postpone a game on account of the weather without specifying what kind of weather would warrant such action. In fact, rules in both leagues allowed the home team owner to determine whether the grounds were fit for ball playing for any game of the season.

Dreyfuss acted in self-interest, of course. Saturday promised a much larger crowd. (Since the clubs split the receipts, the postponement benefited Boston as well.) For Pittsburgh, there was an added dividend. It gave Dreyfuss's finest "artiste" pitcher, Deacon Phillippe, an extra day's rest. It also gave Boston's Cy Young another day's rest. Boosters for both clubs used the day to "nurse their lungs" in anticipation of Saturday's contest. Pirates fans, imitating the Boston contingent, now sported buttons around town that read: "We are all Pittsburgh rooters." They also contracted with a band of their own to rival the Irish band the Royal Rooters had already engaged for game seven. Win or lose, Pirates loyalists made plans to accompany their team to Boston for the finale of the Series.

The main show that gameless Friday, however, was at the state courthouse, where Royal Rooter leaders Mike McGreevey and Charles J. Lavis were on trial for breach of contract. The bandmaster of the Greater Pittsburgh Band, Professor Karl Frederick William Guenther, who sported a waxed mustache and a resplendent uniform to match, claimed that McGreevey and Lavis had contracted the prior Monday for his Italian band's services for four days, not one. The defendants claimed that while they had engaged the band for four days, it was on the condition that their band playing was satisfactory.

McGreevey was not pleased with the band. They would not march around as the Rooters liked to do. They insisted on a bandwagon to carry them back and forth to the park. He paid the bandleader the daily agreed-to price of $90 and told him their services would no longer be needed. The band sued for $270 for the three remaining days of their engagement. After three hours of testimony, the judge, Alderman John Groetzinger, took the case under advisement. Later that morning, he ruled in favor of the Pittsburgh musicians and awarded them $285 in damages and court costs for the breach of contract.

Dreyfuss was correct in his prediction of a financial reward for the Saturday contest. The final game in Pittsburgh produced the largest crowd in the history of the franchise until that time. The Champion Rooters, led by their own forty-piece band—actually, it was Guenther's Greater Pittsburgh Band, the same outfit that had sued McGreevey for breach of contract—had staged a double-line parade five hundred strong from downtown Pittsburgh to the Allegheny and across the bridge to Exposition Park. The march was arranged by Solly Susman, "who is a dyed-in-the-wool, thirty-third-degree fan," said the *Pittsburgh Press*. "In carriages at the head of the procession were another 100 enthusiasts . . . including some of the city's best business men." The rooters twirled their horns and shouted through their megaphones as they made their way from the Seventh Avenue Hotel to Exposition Park. Hundreds more joined the procession as it wound northward. Each rooter wore a large pin with the Pirates' colors—red and navy blue—with gilt letters reading "Loyal Rooters, Pittsburgh, 1903." They cheered: "Phil, Phil, Phillippe, Phil!—He Can Win, and You Bet He Will." The hopes of the Pittsburgh faithful rested on the right arm of the "Steady Man," Deacon Phillippe.

When they arrived at Exposition Park, Pittsburgh's rooters took the special seats the club had reserved for them in section A of the grandstand. Pittsburgh's band was under strict orders to drown out the Boston band's rendition of "Tessie" with "Hail, Hail, the Gang's All Here." Before the game began, Boston's Irish band played "America," and the crowd stood and joined in the chorus. Pittsburgh's band struck up the "Star Spangled Banner" and again all sang. (And, of course, throughout the contest "Tessie" remained the "Hub town favorite.")

The field swelled with 17,038 paid patrons—"a representative crowd . . .

made up of people from all walks of life" including "many lady spectators," reported the *Pittsburgh Gazette*. The Pittsburgh faithful all hoped to send their local heroes back to Boston one game up on their American League rivals. As promised, the steel mills in Homestead and McKeesport closed at noon and granted their workers a half-day holiday to take in the game. Excursion trains filled with spectators had arrived from West Virginia, Ohio, and throughout western Pennsylvania.

Regrettably for the home club, however, Boston returned Cy Young to the mound, and "The Old Roman" would scatter ten hits that produced only three runs. "Rail-splitter Cyrus" had complete control of "both the ball and the batsmen," admitted the *Pittsburgh Gazette*. Meanwhile, the Americans would collect seven runs off Phillippe, who was pitching his fourth complete game of the Series. The *Boston Herald* headline read: "Phillippe Met His Waterloo." Injuries to the Pirates were beginning to mount. Before the game, Captain Clarke was hit on the leg by a bat that flew out of Kitty Bransfield's hands. He never fully recovered his mobility in the Series. Wagner continued to hobble, and the *Pittsburgh Post* admitted that "stars of the Wagner magnitude did not twinkle as much as was desired."

Pittsburgh seemed a disheartened club, having squandered an almost insurmountable three games to one lead in the Series by losing two games in a row in their own park before their enthusiastic fanatics. Finally, Boston's batters had figured out the curves and drops of master hurler Phillippe. The Boston nine faced Phillippe for the fourth time in little over a week. It would be expected that, after a while, they would learn his tricks.

Boston's attack began in the first inning with Collins and Stahl sending the ball into the roped-off crowd in the outfield and earning ground-rule triples. They both would score. Boston added another two runs in the fourth on two more triples by Freeman and Ferris. In all there were seven triples hit by the two clubs that day, a World Series record that still stands.

When Deacon Phillippe came to bat in the bottom of the third inning, a contingent of the Pittsburgh faithful approached their star and presented him with a diamond pin in thanks for his superb effort in the Series. The game was stopped momentarily as players on both squads crowded around to see the sparkling prize. The Boston Americans joined the Pirates in congratulating the great twirler. When the game resumed, Deacon singled sharply to left, but nothing came of it. Pittsburgh fought back with single runs in the fourth, sixth, and ninth innings, but it was too little too late. By a score of 7–3, the Boston Americans took their first lead in the Series, four games to three in a game completed in one hour, forty-five minutes.

GAME 7

Team	1	2	3	4	5	6	7	8	9	R	H	E
Boston	2	0	0	2	0	2	0	1	0	7	11	4
Pittsburgh	0	0	0	1	0	1	0	0	1	3	10	3

The Royal Rooters marched back to the Monongahela House led by their Irish band and bid farewell to Pittsburgh. By all reports, they had enjoyed their sojourn in the Smoky City, although many commented that they could have done without the smoke and dirt in the air. Mike McGreevey, Charles Lavis, and Michael Rogan, on behalf of the Royal Rooters, visited the headquarters of the *Pittsburgh Press* and left the following notice to be printed:

> The Boston rooters hereby thank *The Press* for its considerate treatment and for the fairness displayed toward the Boston club during its stay in Pittsburgh. They hope the relations between the Boston and Pittsburgh rooters may ever be as cordial as they are now.

Lined up in a double row, each carrying a dress suitcase, the Royal Rooters headed to the station and boarded the train heading north out of the Smoky City toward Buffalo, then east to Boston. Some five hundred Pittsburgh rooters escorted them to the train. "The sidewalks were jammed along the route of march and never before has a visiting crowd of rooters got the cordial send-off that was given the Boston boys."

The Boston players boarded the train "as happy as school boys out for their first game of marbles in the spring." Pittsburgh rooters and their base-ball club boarded the same train, set to arrive in Boston by Sunday night. They were in a very different mood, however, unhappy about their perfor-mance and their prospects. The *Pittsburgh Press* reported that the players "were not in the best of spirits, for the defeat they suffered at the hands of the Bostons has somewhat discouraged them." When the Pirates finally arrived at the Vendome Hotel in Boston, an unknown Boston prankster had left Pittsburgh stars Wagner and Phillippe free copies of the *American Undertaker* magazine.

THE SOLOMON FAMILY

Millions of immigrants from Europe and Asia
came to America in the decades surrounding the
turn of the twentieth century. Baer Solomon's family
moved from Kiev in the Pale of Russia to settle
in the South End of Boston, where young Samuel
would learn to love baseball, America's Game.

A New Jewish Homeland:
The Great Migration

Samuel Solomon, a future baseball fanatic, was born in Kiev, Russia, in 1890. Located in Ukraine on the hilly west bank of the Dnieper River, the ancient city of Kiev grew to economic prominence at the crossroads on the trade routes between the Baltic and the Mediterranean. On Volodymyrska Street stood the Russian Orthodox Cathedral of St. Sophia, built in the eleventh century by Prince Yaroslav the Wise. Jews had lived in Kiev as early as the tenth century, but they were outsiders to Ukrainian social life. The Jewish laws had always imposed restrictions on their economic and social prospects. Nonetheless, by the end of the nineteenth century, Kiev had become a center of Jewish literature and learning, the home of Shalom Aleichem.

Sam's father, Baer, was known as a scholar of the Talmud, the writing of the rabbis through the ages that interpreted the ambiguous phrases of the Hebrew Bible. He rose from bookkeeper to manager of a sugar refining business that was owned by "secret Jews," those who hid their faith in order to carry out their commercial businesses. When his employers asked Baer to prepare their sons for bar mitzvah, he agreed to do so, keeping their secret. At least once a week and sometimes more, the Solomon family attended the Kiev *schul*, the synagogue in their Podil neighborhood.

Life was tolerable for those Jews who were permitted to live in the city away from the grim life of the shtetl. Sam attended the Gymnasium, a private elementary school. Baer first felt the sting of anti-Semitism when the owners of the sugar refinery sent him to another province to establish a new plant. He returned home and announced that they could not live in a country that permitted, and even fostered, such hatred. He was off to the "New Land," he said, "to America." He set out alone in 1899, promising to send for his family.

Baer Solomon traveled across America and liked what he saw. He settled finally in Brooklyn, near fellow countrymen from Kiev. A year later he sent for two of his sons, Nathan and Louis. The two boys were met at Ellis Island by the Hebrew Immigrant Aid Society (HIAS). Starting in 1892, HIAS assisted immigrants in adjusting to their new environment by meeting arrivals at the ship, placing them with relatives, and assuring temporary accommodations when necessary.

The boys knew only that their father used the General Post Office in Brooklyn as his address and that he would go to pick up his mail twice a week. Nathan and Louis sat on the front steps of the Brooklyn post office with their names on signs around their necks waiting for their father to find them, which he did.

Seeking better business prospects, Baer moved to Boston with Nathan and Louis and sent for his wife, young Sam, and his daughters. They arrived in America in 1901. The family was together again, living in a tenement on Hampden Street in Boston's South End, the only Jewish family in an Irish neighborhood. Baer took on steady work as the first superintendent of the Hebrew Home for the Aged, now called the Hebrew Rehabilitation Center.

Sam, who could speak no English, faced a daunting challenge as an eleven-year-old in a new country. He attended the Dearborn Grammar School in Roxbury, an area of Boston adjoining the South End that was soon to become home to Jewish immigrants who were moving out of Boston's North End. During his school years, Sam Solomon discovered his lifelong passion — baseball.

Within walking distance of Sam's home and his school were two major league ballparks—the Walpole Street Grounds, also called the South End Grounds, where the National League Beaneaters (later renamed the Braves) played their home games, and the new Huntington Avenue Grounds, home to the American League club. After school, Sam would sneak into the ballpark to watch his heroes play. On some days, the clubs would offer free admission to anyone younger than ten who came with his or her father. In order to see his favorite pastime, Sam Solomon adopted many "fathers" on their way to the ticket booth.

By 1903, Sam Solomon had learned English and baseball. For years to come he would regale his children with stories of the first World Series. Cy Young, Honus Wagner, Jimmy Collins, Fred Clarke—he saw them all play as he attended every home game without buying one ticket. There weren't many Jews who were so enraptured by baseball. It was seen as an Irish game, but Sam lived in an Irish neighborhood and his buddies were young Irish boys. His pals called him "The Duke" because he dressed so well.

Sam graduated from grammar school and started at Boston's English High School (America's first public high school, founded in 1821), but he did not finish. He found work in the garment industry, first as a delivery boy and as a fabric cutter. He moved to better jobs in the industry and by age twenty-three had started his own company on Harrison Avenue, where he would eventually employ two hundred stitchers to make ladies' petticoats. But there always was baseball, and Sam Solomon, business owner, would sneak out of work in time to see the first pitch at 3:00 P.M.

One might imagine the pride Sam felt when his cousin Moe Solomon became a professional baseball player in the New York Giants organization. The Giants were always interested in Jewish ballplayers who could appeal to Jewish patrons at New York's Polo Grounds. The Giants publicized him as the "Rabbi of Swat" in order to compete for the public's attention toward Babe Ruth, the "Sultan of Swat," who played across town. Moe Solomon had an impressive minor league career, stroking forty-nine homers in 108 games in the Class C Southwestern League. Moe had little more than a cup of tea in the major leagues, however. In 1923, he played two games at the end of the season, collecting three hits in eight at bats for an impressive .375 lifetime batting average, with one double and one RBI.

Baer Solomon passed away in 1921 and never knew his grandson Bernard, born in 1923 and called "Bunny" throughout his life, a fond appellation applied almost at birth. When his aunt first saw him as a baby, she said, "Oh, what a cute little bunny," and the name stuck. Bunny would inherit his father's devotion to baseball, playing ten hours a day when he could. He joined organized teams that wore uniforms, and his father bought him a pair of spikes, which he showed off by parading around the neighborhood. Bunny was never so proud as when his father left work to watch him play baseball.

The Jews of Boston

In October 1903, most members of Boston's Jewish community attended services on the High Holidays, as they did every year whether they were second-generation Reformed Jews from Germany or first-generation Orthodox Jews recently arrived from eastern Europe. Yom Kippur, starting with the appearance of the first star the evening before and the chanting of the Kol Nidre, was the holiest day of the Jewish year. A solemn night and day of fasting followed. Yom Kippur coincided that year with the first game of the World Series.

The history of Jews in Boston can be traced back through the seventeenth century. Until the 1850s, however, the Jewish population was comparatively small because no Jewish cemetery was allowed in Massachusetts until that time. With the nearest cemeteries in Albany and Newport, no observant Jew would settle in the Boston area for fear that he could not be buried according to Jewish law within a day of his death.

Most of the Jewish immigrants arrived during the second half of the nineteenth century and the first decades of the twentieth century. The first Jews to arrive came from Germany. For the most part, these German immigrants felt comfortable in the urban environment. They arrived with skills and some resources. German Jews assimilated with comparative ease into

Boston's evolving economy. The waves of Jewish refugees from Poland and Russia that would arrive after 1880, however, faced far greater challenges.

The daily Boston press respectfully reported the Jewish holy religious events in 1903. Rabbi Hirshberg, assisted by Cantor Walkowitz, led the Yom Kippur services at Ohabei Shalom (Lovers of Peace), Boston's oldest congregation formed more than a half-century earlier. Rabbi Fleischer of the rival Temple Adath Israel delivered a sermon entitled "How Far Are We 'Civilized'?" Rabbi Fleischer, who had completed a decade of leadership of the German-Jewish congregation, worried that "our boasted civilization was only skin deep." He urged his congregants toward collective self-criticism as a "habit . . . to be encouraged." The rabbi's broad focus encompassed the ills of the modern world:

> I may not, though a loyal American, approve of all the domestic or foreign doings of my country, but I need not, because conscious of my country's crime, be silent before the evident misdeeds of other peoples. Indeed conscience demands the condemnation of both.

Rabbi Fleischer expressed his outrage at the heinous lynching of American blacks, at Turkish atrocities against their Armenian countrymen, and at Russian barbarities against landless peasants, including his fellow Jews. Only by controlling the "savage within," Rabbi Fleischer preached, could mankind make progress toward genuine civilization.

In 1903, the millions of Jews who remained in Russia were continuing to experience the czarist savagery firsthand. The bloody pogroms—private murder and mayhem under official sanction—were a repeated, but unpredictable, curse. These onslaughts made stable life in the Jewish villages, the shtetl, contingent on the whims of others. In Kishinev, near Kiev, during Passover in April 1903, a mob of Gentiles killed forty-nine Jews and injured five hundred more. The Warsaw newspaper *Hazefira* reported that "the men kept murdering not only as if possessed, but also with indifference, as in a slaughterhouse."

When word of this latest atrocity reached Boston, the Jews of the city gathered at Faneuil Hall on May 19, 1903, to express their pain and outrage. A *Boston Globe* editorial on May 28, 1903, explained to its readers that events like the Kishinev massacre were the reason that the Jews of Russia had emigrated to America.

For a thousand years, life for the Jews living outside of Israel in the Diaspora had fluctuated between the tolerable and the unbearable. Invited to migrate to eastern Europe in the thirteenth century by Boleslav the Pious, the king of Poland, Jews cultivated the growth of a mercantile system in the agrarian society. This shift eastward mitigated the terror many Jews suffered in parts of western Europe where they were accused of poisoning streams and wells and even of causing the Black Death.

By the nineteenth century, most of Poland had fallen under Russian czarist rule. In order to separate her Jews from the rest of the population, Catherine the Great had ordered them confined to the villages and towns of "the Pale of Settlement," a 386,000-square-mile region stretching from the Baltic to the Black Sea, including parts of Poland, Lithuania, Belarus, and Ukraine. By the end of the nineteenth century, the Pale was home to almost five million Jews. Most were required to live in the shtetls, villages romanticized in the stories of Sholom Aleichem (and on Broadway in *Fiddler on the Roof*). In reality, they were barren collections of medieval huts with dirt floors and mud thoroughfares surrounding a central marketplace and a single synagogue. Life was primitive. Most men worked as artisans and craftsmen—tanners, tailors, bakers, cobblers, carpenters, blacksmiths, furriers—or as small traders. Most women cared for the house and the children, while other women attended to the religious bath, the *mikvah,* or served as matchmakers for arranged marriages or as feather-pluckers collecting feathers to use in pillows.

The Jews of the Pale disciplined their lives with religious rituals. Religious instruction was a male responsibility in the old country. The universal language of the eastern European Jews was Yiddish, an amalgam of Middle High German, Russian, Polish, and Hebrew. Very few people in the shtetl spoke Russian, and only boys who attended school in the cheder learned to read Hebrew.

Throughout the nineteenth century, the Jews of Russia experienced alternating periods of sufferance and repression. Czar Nicholas I instituted conscription for males between the ages of twelve and eighteen for fifteen years of service in the army. Few conscripts ever survived to return home. In 1851, Russia enacted The Temporary Rules Concerning the Assortment of Jews that divided Jewish workers into five classifications: guild merchants, petty traders, artisans, laborers, and unemployed idlers, called luftmenschen by their fellow Jews and an accepted part of shtetl society. Jews were forbidden from participating in any other occupations.

Czar Alexander II's reign brought a period of toleration. Military service was reduced to six years. In the 1880s, however, after Alexander's assassination by a group of nihilists who had been living in the home of a Jewish woman, oppression returned under Alexander III in the form of exclusionary laws and practices. The Jews were prohibited from owning or renting land outside their towns. Jewish children were excluded from government schools. Jews were prohibited from traveling. Violence against Jews mounted by Gentile mobs under official protection, the pogroms, periodically drew blood and rained destruction.

News about America came to the shtetl through newspapers. Those who could read shared the glowing reports of the new golden land. Not surprisingly, the positive news was exaggerated, since the steamship lines wrote many of the stories, looking to induce passengers to travel across the Atlantic. Who would undertake such an unthinkable journey of thousands of miles to a land where they did not speak the language or know the customs? They had a choice to stay—and most did—but at least in America the killing of Jews was not an officially sanctioned government policy.

A collection of essays about Boston immigrants published in 1903, *Americans in Process: A Settlement Study,* edited by Robert A. Woods, although a mostly sympathetic narrative about Jewish immigrants to Boston, occasionally spews the anti-Semitic tone of the times. While acknowledging that the "emigration of Jews from Russia has been indirectly necessitated by the repressive action of the Russian government," Woods blames the Jews for their own plight:

> The real cause of the trouble lies in the long and bitter contest which has gone on in that country between Jew and Gentile. At last many of the Gentiles, finding themselves undermined by the subtle Jewish methods, organized riots and destroyed the property of those who, they felt, had undone them. . . . The Russian peasant was, of course, no match for the Jews in the instinct for sharp practice in trade. Even hedged in by a multitude of restrictions, the Jews have become an economic power in Russia—too often a grasping and relentless power. If they had perfect freedom, they would erelong control the material resources of the country. [The czar] feels that the Jew must not be allowed to outwit them and hinder their natural economic development.

Later in his text, however, Woods concludes that the "Jewish race has an immemorial record as the prolific mother of genius," a key element in the development of a "better social order" in America.

Between 1880 and 1914, two million eastern European Jews would come to the "Goldene Medina," the Golden Land of America. Although their living conditions were meager both in Russia and in America, they came hoping for opportunity. They left behind what had been for centuries their homeland. Life was intolerable in a country where Jews enjoyed no rights and were subject to unspeakable crimes without recourse. The draft, the pogroms, rampant disease, and periodic famine motivated many to leave friends and family behind and trek westward.

Young male Jews were the first to move. They traveled initially to the slums of Minsk, Vilna, Warsaw, and Bialystok looking for work, but those would only be way stations on their journey west. They would soon be on their way to western Europe, then to German ports where they boarded ships that would take them to America.

Without passports or papers, Jews crossed international borders by bribing guards stationed along the well-established routes. They would walk to the border-crossing points when railway travel was not available or affordable. Arriving at the northern German ports of Hamburg and Bremen, they would travel to America in steerage for as little as $15 a ticket.

Fathers such as Baer Solomon came first to find work. They would save money in order to send their wives and children a *shiffscarte* (steamship ticket). Conditions aboard ship were thoroughly unpleasant. As many as two thousand sailed steerage, packed in the underbelly of the vessel adjoining the steering mechanisms. There was little air or ventilation but abundant seasickness and head lice. Maintaining Kosher strictures added to the immigrants' challenge. Jews aboard ship would live for days on herring, bread, and tea. It took from ten to seventeen days to make the transatlantic crossing.

The process of assimilation for Jews into American society began immediately, often even before arrival at the port of entry. Names too difficult to spell were changed on the ship's manifest. (Stories about immigration officials Americanizing names are legend.) Arriving at Castle Garden in New York (later replaced by a new facility on Ellis Island) or at the East Boston Immigration Building, the immigrants again faced men in uniform. These immigration officials looked very much like the border guards they had had to bribe on their way west. Only a few Jewish immigrants were turned away, however. Arriving with little more than a few dollars, facing for the first time a city with tall buildings, streetcars, and electric lights, is it any wonder the immigrants were uneasy? This whole new world was strange indeed!

Life in Boston

Most eastern European Jews who came to Boston lived in the tenements of the North End, the same buildings in crowded neighborhoods occupied by the Irish immigrants a half-century earlier. The dwellings had no hot water or bathtubs and but one toilet in the building or the yard. The North End provided the cheapest housing in the city in close proximity to the Hanover Street business district. Although the North End was predominantly

Jewish and Italian, at the turn of the century representatives of twenty-five different nationalities, some twenty-eight thousand inhabitants, populated the area. As Robert A. Woods wrote in 1903, the North End was "Boston's classic land of poverty."

As Russian Jews later spread out to East Boston and the West End (where they became the predominant immigrant group) and then to the South End and Roxbury, new Italian immigrants would supplant them in the North End neighborhoods surrounding Hanover Street. The North End would remain predominantly Italian throughout the twentieth century.

The German-Jewish immigrants who had arrived in Boston before 1880 had dispersed around the city by the time the waves of Russian immigrants began arriving. They had brought with them from southwestern Germany a reformist attitude toward their faith and its customs. They had settled mainly in the South End, and a few wealthy Jewish merchants even bought town houses in the fashionable Back Bay. The largely assimilated community of German Jews was shocked at the arrival of their co-religionists. The very appearance of the Russian Jews embarrassed them. With beards and earlocks, their Orthodox religious piety conflicted with the reform movement the German Jews had adopted as their own. Many within the German-Jewish population, however, recognized the need to help their Russian "cousins." Although for generations German and Russian Jews would live, work, and pray separately, the settled and assimilated Jews formed charitable organizations to assist the new settlers. The Combined Jewish Philanthropies, founded in Boston in 1895 by, among others, Boston lawyer Louis Brandeis, was the first federated charity in the nation. It would serve as a model upon which all other federations, such as the United Way and the Community Chest, would be based. Beth Israel Hospital was established in 1916 on Townsend Street in Roxbury, in part because Jewish medical students could not get internships at other Boston hospitals.

The new Russian immigrants soon learned that it was essential to appear to assimilate quickly. As recently arrived greenhorns, they were subject to harassment. Women quickly discarded their wigs (the *sheitel*), and men replaced their long black frock coats and shaved their beards. The attitudes of the new immigrants fostered a rapid acculturation. They took pride in becoming reputable and respected Americans. Religion was a steadying influence in their lives, but assimilation was imperative. Although a public school education risked undermining religious orthodoxy, it was avidly pursued. To the surprise of many rabbis, the second generation of Jewish immigrants did not convert to Protestantism despite exposure to other religions.

In the public schools, the children of the Jewish immigrants learned a new language and absorbed new habits and culture. Caroline S. Atherton and Elizabeth Y. Rutan, two Brahmin workers in the immigrant settlement houses, examined the plenary importance of this public schooling on students of an impressionable age:

> Enthusiasm is found everywhere among the instructors of foreign children, and with it is a corresponding fervor of belief in the ability of their pupils, especially the Hebrews, who are said to rush through the grades as soon as they get the language. . . . [T]he school practically dictates the conduct of the child during his waking hours.

Devoted North End schoolteachers brought to life their own proverb: "Land on Saturday, settle on Sunday, school on Monday, vote on Tuesday." Many debated the essential function of the grammar school. Bernard Ruskin wrote that he was

> weary of seeing the subject of education treated as if education meant only teaching children to write and cipher. The real education, the only education which should be compulsory, means nothing of the kind; it means teaching children to be clean, active, honest and useful.

The Boston public school curriculum certainly met Ruskin's aspirations. It was filled with moral training, physical education, and manual training, as well as a weekly bath offered to students at the Paul Revere School in the North End. Land was set aside next to schools to serve as playgrounds.

In the evening, Boston's public schools were filled with hundreds of adult immigrants thirsting to learn both the language and the customs of their new land. They came directly from work without supper and squeezed into seats designed for children. They would leave with a new pride in their adopted country and a sense that economic progress was inevitable for all those who made the effort.

The Peddlers

Many Jewish male immigrants first earned a living by "taking a basket" and becoming peddlers, a variation of shtetl trading conducted in the old country. They filled their baskets on credit with supplies that Jewish, Irish, and Yankee customers would buy. Among the first English sentences these newly arrived street capitalists would learn was "Look in the basket."

The economic ladder among street merchants was well established. A successful basket peddler might have the resources to carry a "pack on the back" filled with linens and dresses that he would take to boardinghouses to sell. A tin peddler would add kitchen utensils to his pack, and a horse-and-buggy trader could carry more merchandise and travel farther to sell his wares. At the top of the street merchant ladder was the custom peddler, who would carry only samples, accept orders for new dresses, and then, after delivery of the goods, collect payment in installments. A successful peddler might accumulate enough capital to purchase a small store and supply other peddlers with their merchandise.

Commerce flourished on crowded Hanover Street in the North End. Jessie Fremont Beale and Anne Worthington, who worked in the settlement house, described the scene:

> While there is much of peculiar interest in Jewish life, there can be, where there is so much squalor, but little beauty. On the streets the commercial instinct is everywhere evident. The dan-

gling old clothes, the pawnshop windows filled with everything that could possibly be turned into money, the baskets, barrels and carts of foul-smelling fish do not add to the charm of the scene, and are hardly offset by the boxes of green vegetables and ripe fruits which border the sidewalk; but the human element, the owners of the shops and wagons, with their forlorn expressions of anxiety to sell, the patriarchal old men, the . . . purchasing housekeepers and the energetic young salesmen who do not hesitate to drag customers into the shops, are of never-ending interest. The general dinginess of the locality is perhaps centered in the unattractive Jewish restaurants and meat shops [that] contrast strangely with the occasional corner or basement where second-hand Hebrew books are sold, and where beautiful parchment and leather bindings tempt one to dream of their scholarly past. Fine old candlesticks are often for sale in these places. It is to such bits of brightness that this region owes much of its small aspect of cheer.

Although many Jewish immigrants had to work in factories, few performed simple manual labor and most sought to be free from control by Gentile owners as soon as they could. They valued independence, even with its economic uncertainty and risk. Jewish women immigrants worked in mills and factories, many operating sewing machines in the garment industries. Unlike Irish immigrant girls, Jewish women (like Greek and Italian women) rarely performed domestic work outside their homes. At night, immigrant homes were turned into piecework factories in which all members of the family worked.

In the Jewish immigrant neighborhoods of Boston, there was a network of private charities and settlement houses offering emergency relief, counseling, employment opportunities, and cultural classes in American life. Mutual aid societies offered financial and moral support, and adult school provided classes in English.

And then there was baseball. For the Jewish immigrant, baseball represented the most American of pastimes. Nothing like this game was played in the Pale of Russia, although the Jewish sacred book, the Talmud, does contain favorable references to ball games.

Crowds—including Boston's Jews—would gather to witness these athletic spectacles. For the price of admission they could spend a few hours rooting with their fellow Americans. Abraham Cahan, for decades the editor of the leading Yiddish newspaper, the *Daily Forward,* wrote an advice column answering inquiries from his readers. In 1903, Cahan received a letter from an immigrant who objected to the fact that his son played baseball with his friends from public school. Cahan responded: "It is a mistake to keep children locked up in the house. Bring them up to be educated, ethical and decent, but also to be physically strong, so that they should not feel inferior. . . . Mainly, let us not so raise the children that they should grow up foreigners in their own birthplace." This game of baseball, Cahan wrote, was a perfect way to give Jewish boys a link to their fellow countrymen "without demanding a sacrifice of Jewish beliefs and tradition."

Jews and Baseball

Any discussion of the connection of Jews with professional baseball normally begins (and may end) with the stories of the great modern Jewish ballplayers—Hall of Famers Hank Greenberg and Sandy Koufax. (Perhaps some might add the Red Sox catcher Moe Berg to the list, but not because of his baseball-playing abilities. Berg, the son of Russian immigrants and a brilliant lawyer who spoke many languages, spied for the Office of Strategic Services during World War II.)

For more than 150 years, Jews have been involved in both the business and the playing of our national game. The current commissioner of baseball, Bud Selig, and the great leader of the players' union, Marvin Miller, are both Jewish. But the influence of Jewish immigrants and their sons on the game—both good and bad—goes deep into the history of the national pastime. For example, while Jack Norworth wrote the lyrics to the game's anthem, "Take Me Out to the Ball Game," it was Jewish immigrant Albert Von Tilzer who composed the music.

In the earliest days of the game, the son of a Jewish immigrant, Lipman Emanuel Pike, known as "The Iron Batter," was among baseball's first professional ballplayers. Pike began playing organized baseball one week after his bar mitzvah. In 1866, he was offered $20 a week to play for the Philadelphia Athletics. On July 16, 1866, he reportedly hit six home runs, five in succession, in a 67–25 Athletics trouncing of the crosstown Alert Club of Philadelphia. A good hitter and base runner, Pike played for various clubs for the next decade, then joined St. Louis for the inaugural National League season. Over his next five seasons in the National League and the American Association, Pike averaged .304. He then completed his seventeen-year career in the majors as a manager.

The National League's most powerful owner at the turn of the twentieth century was a despicable character named Andrew Freedman, a New York City lawyer and crony of Boss Richard Croker and his politicos of Tammany Hall. A handsome bachelor of German-Jewish ancestry, Freedman became rich by speculating on real estate, and not always on the legitimate side of the ledger. Freedman ran the New York Giants from 1895 until 1902, during which time he hired and fired sixteen managers. He was arrogant, overbearing, and insufferable. *New York World* observed that Freedman had "an astonishing faculty for making enemies." He barred from the Polo Grounds reporters who had criticized him and even punched a reporter from the *New York Times* in the jaw. In 1900, Freedman had twenty-two libel suits pending against the *New York Sun*. By all accounts, he was a loathsome character, without tact or social graces.

Freedman's most celebrated on-field incident demonstrates how Jews were considered at the turn of the century. Freedman had disposed of James "Ducky" Holmes in a cash sale to St. Louis. Upon Holmes's return to the Polo Grounds, the outfielder was greeted with jeers by the spectators. He responded: "At least I don't have to work for no Sheeny anymore!" Freedman rushed the field accompanied by his private guards to remove Holmes from the premises. The umpire ruled the game forfeited by the Giants, and the National League fined both Freedman and Holmes. *Sporting News* could not understand the penalty to Ducky Holmes: "Insulting the Hebrew race," it wrote, "was a trifling offense." Any penalty would be a "perversion of justice."

Off the field, Freedman schemed to syndicate the national game. In 1901, at his estate in Red Bank, New Jersey, Freedman conspired with a clique of eastern National League owners to restructure the circuit as the National Baseball Trust. Ownership of the eight teams would be pooled with shares in the trust distributed unequally to the magnates based on the value of their individual clubs. (Freedman would own the most shares under his plan.) A board of regents that Freedman controlled would manage the entire enterprise. Albert Spalding, the great baseball entrepreneur of the nineteenth century, rallied the western club owners, in particular Barney Dreyfuss of Pittsburgh, against Freedman's assault on baseball's tradition of individual ownership. In the process, Spalding forced the Tammany Hall lieutenant out of baseball. Upon Freedman's death, *Sporting News* wrote, "He had an arbitrary disposition, a violent temper, and an ungovernable tongue in anger which was easily provoked, and he was disposed to be arbitrary to the point of tyranny with subordinates."

By comparison to Freedman's negative influence on the sport, his Jewish contemporary Barney Dreyfuss must be recognized as one of the most progressive owners in baseball's development as the national game. Born Bernhard Dreyfuss in Freiburg, Germany, in 1865, the future baseball entrepreneur had modest aspirations. His father, Samuel Dreyfuss, had immigrated to America in 1850, settling in Kentucky, where he established a dry goods business. In 1861, however, Samuel Dreyfuss returned to Freiburg because of ill health. His son Bernhard studied accounting as an apprentice in a bank in Karlsruhe, Germany. In 1881, two of his first cousins, the Bernheims, enticed Dreyfuss to immigrate to America and work in their liquor business in Kentucky. Bernhard Americanized his first name to "Barney" and worked as a bookkeeper in the Bernheims' profitable distillery in the western Kentucky town of Paducah. (Years later Dreyfuss would claim that he began work with the Bernheims by scrubbing whiskey barrels, a tale the Bernheims did not corroborate. In his autobiography, Isaac Bernheim recalls Barney Dreyfuss as "exceedingly apt, though at times a somewhat careless young fellow.") The Bernheims moved their distillery to Louisville in 1888, where it does business today as Heavenly Hill Distilleries and produces J. W. Dant bourbon, among other spirits.

Isaac Bernheim promoted Dreyfuss to head bookkeeper and "credit man" when the business relocated to Louisville and offered his cousin an interest in the enterprise. Bernheim notes in his autobiography that after leaving the firm Barney enjoyed "decided success" as principal owner of the Pittsburgh Baseball Club. By 1910, Bernheim commented, Dreyfuss was "very happily married and the father of an interesting family" in Pittsburgh. In fact, Dreyfuss had established himself as one of Pittsburgh's civic leaders. His benevolence toward his players was well known. Most important for our purposes, German-Jewish Barney Dreyfuss created the first World Series.

Americanization

Life for Jews in America was infinitely better than in the Old World. With access to free public education, Jews flourished as businessmen and professionals. For some, such as young Samuel Solomon, American baseball became a passion that would not be stilled in adulthood. There were many "Samuel Solomons" in America's cities, immigrants who quickly adopted the customs and pastimes of their new land. For others, such as Barney Dreyfuss, baseball became a profitable enterprise. As a result of his ownership of the Pirates, Dreyfuss became a respected solon of Pittsburgh. Never more important than family, community, and faith, baseball remained a vital element in the new life Jewish immigrants made for themselves in this country.

THE BOSTON AMERICANS AND THE PITTSBURGH PIRATES

*The twenty-eight participants of the first World
Series included Boston's Cy Young (second row,
sixth from the left) and Pittsburgh's Honus Wagner
(third row, first from the right). Their legacy is
the annual fall classic that brings closure to a
long season of play on the diamonds of America.
They were talented young men whose fame was
fleeting. The object of adoration one day, they
might be discarded by management the next.*

Boston Victorious:
The World Series Tradition

Poor Doheny

With the teams in transit from the west, the Boston newspapers were filled with glowing predictions of the certain victory that lay ahead for the American League club. There was one disturbing newspaper story, however, that reminded the baseball world that their heroes were mortal. The press reported that Edward Doheny, Pittsburgh's splendid left-handed pitcher for most of the season, had gone "berserk."

Weeks earlier Doheny had vanished from the Pittsburgh club, claiming he was being pursued by detectives. Doheny's brother, a priest, located him and escorted him to their home in Andover, Massachusetts, just north of Boston near the New Hampshire border. It was hoped that rest and recuperation would cure his illness. Doheny's teammates "attributed his queerness to a nervous breakdown as a result of worry over his pitching." He tried to return to the team but was soon back in Andover under the care of a physician, Dr. E. C. Conroy.

Doheny's teammates, hoping to brighten his attitude, sent him his Pirates uniform. Apparently Doheny was confused by the gesture, thinking the club needed his services. The Pirates could certainly have used another strong arm to complement Deacon Phillippe, but Doheny was in no condition to compete.

The newspapers reported that on Saturday evening, October 10, Doheny forcibly ejected Dr. Conroy from his house, saying that "he did not need his attentions any longer." Early Sunday morning, Doheny attacked Oberlin Howarth, his "faith cure doctor and nurse," with an iron stove poker, rendering him bloodied and unconscious. Doheny then "smashed things right and left." Doheny's wife rushed to the neighbors for assistance. Dressed in his nightclothes at the doorway to his house and armed with the iron poker, Doheny held off the police for an hour with threats to kill the first man who approached him. Finally overpowered by the police, Doheny was taken to the police station where, under the direction of Judge Andrew C. Stone, two doctors pronounced him insane. That afternoon, he was committed to the Danvers Asylum for the Criminally Insane.

When the Pittsburgh captain, Fred Clarke, arrived at Boston's Vendome Hotel and was asked about "poor Doheny," he said that Doheney had been a real favorite among the boys. "We all feel sorry for poor Doheny. . . . If we had had Doheny in the box . . . the standing would now be Pittsburgh 5; Boston 1." Clarke said the cause of Doheney's "high nervous disorder" was "overwork." Doheny would never play professional baseball again.

A cheering crowd of five hundred loyalists had greeted Jimmy Collins and his Boston boys when they stepped onto the train platform that Sunday afternoon at South Station. All looked tired from the long journey and ready to finish the Series as quickly as possible. Heavy rain caused the postponement of Monday's game, giving the players an extra day to recover from the tiring train trip and the arduous four games played in Pittsburgh. The *Pittsburgh Gazette* characterized the weather as "typically Bostonian—rainy, squally, and generally wretched." While most of the Pirates tried to stay warm at the Vendome Hotel, captain Fred Clarke took advantage of the day off to visit Mrs. Doheny in Andover, and Barney Dreyfuss promised that he would provide for the pitcher's wife. That evening the Pirate players attended the performance of *The Yankee Consul* at the Tremont Theatre as guests of Barney Dreyfuss, who had seen the show on his earlier visit to Boston after the first game of the Series.

The Eighth—and Final—Game

On October 13, 1903, a cold, dark, and overcast day in Boston, the eighth and final game of the first World Series was played at the Huntington Avenue Grounds. Scalpers could fetch $3 for a $1 ticket as they hawked their wares in front of George Wright's sports emporium in downtown Boston. The "hotel sharks," the *Pittsburgh Gazette* reported, demanded $4.50 for the same ticket. None were to be had at the Grounds box office.

Pirates stars Honus Wagner and Fred Clarke, who would later be inducted into baseball's Hall of Fame, were nursing injuries. Wagner told Pittsburgh reporters that both his arms were "gone," and he would not play ball the following year. (Wagner annually made these end-of-season threats of retirement.) When the gong sounded, however, both stars were ready for the contest.

The Pirates had traveled east with a band of their most loyal rooters, including James L. Orris, the proprietor of the Carnegie Hotel and a long-time friend of Honus Wagner. The sportswriters of Pittsburgh, including John H. Gruber of the *Pittsburgh Post* and Frank McQuiston of the *Pittsburgh Dispatch*, were also on hand for the finale in Boston. Following the example of Boston's Royal Rooters who had traveled to the Smoky City, the Pittsburgh faithful had engaged a local band "that assures an excellent musical programme," said the *Pittsburgh Press*. "Discouraged though they would be, the Pirates will put up a great fighting game."

The Royal Rooters had hired the Boston Letter Carriers Band to entertain, and once again "Tessie" was the preferred song. As the *Boston Herald* reported, "in Pittsburgh it was 'Tessie' when the games went favorably, 'Tessie' if a player made a hit, and 'Tessie' when a good catch was made." There were only 7,455 fans in attendance at the Huntington Avenue

Grounds for the eighth game, although years later many more than that would claim to have watched that final contest. The speculators who had purchased tickets in anticipation of a handy profit were the big losers for game eight.

The newspapers reported that Edward Martyn was among the fans in attendance. Martyn was a noted Irish playwright and a wealthy Catholic activist. He was born in County Galway in 1859 and was educated at Oxford. His home—Tullira Castle in Ardrahan—had been in his family for centuries. Martyn was a major contributor to the Irish literary renaissance of the time, along with William Butler Yeats, George Moore, and Lady Augusta Gregory. In 1899, they founded the Irish Literary Theatre in Dublin, where Martyn's play *The Heather Field,* filled with Ibsen-like social realism, was among the first produced.

Bill Dineen, Boston's World Series hero, would hurl a four-hit, eight-strikeout shutout of the Pirates, winning his third game (and second shutout) of the Series against one loss. The 1903 Series was clearly the highlight of Dineen's career. It was his only appearance in postseason play. During the 1904 season, however, Dineen set a major league record by pitching thirty-seven consecutive complete games in thirty-seven starts, and the following season, on September 27, 1905, he pitched a no-hitter for Boston. Traded to the St. Louis Browns midway in the 1907 season for $1,000 and Albert "Beanie" Jacobsen (a left-hander who would never get into a game for Boston), Dineen completed his twelve-year major league career with a 170–177 win-loss record. After retiring from the mound, Dineen became a celebrated American League umpire. A respected arbiter, he called balls and strikes for twenty-nine years and umpired in forty-five World Series games.

Deacon Phillippe took the mound once again for the Pirates and pitched his fifth complete game of the World Series, a record that still stands. He sustained the final and deciding loss for the National Leaguers. In total, Phillippe had a most extraordinary Series. He walked only three batters in his five games and struck out twenty in forty-four innings of work. He had won all three of the Pirates' victories. (Boston's Bill Dineen also won three games, making the 1903 World Series the only Series in history when two pitchers won three games each.) Phillippe would have one more opportunity to pitch in a World Series, during the Pirates' successful 1909 contest against the Detroit Tigers, but he was relegated to only two brief relief appearances in games that the Pirates lost. In his thirteen years in the majors, however, the Deacon never had a losing season, finishing with 189 career wins against 107 losses.

Dineen was in command from the start of the game, retiring the first eleven batters before walking Leach and giving up a single to Wagner in the fourth, but no damage was done. Captain Fred Clarke appeared to be "lame, but game." Meanwhile, Boston scored two runs in the bottom of the fourth frame, the big hit a Freeman triple that let the Royal Rooters' "throats run riot." The Americans added a third run in the sixth on a triple by Lachance, but Dineen would not need the extra help. He was in control. In the top of the ninth, Clarke and Leach flied out. The *Boston Post* captured the excitement of the last out:

> It fell to the great Honus Wagner, premier batsman of the National League, to make the last protest against Boston's claim to the world's championship, and as the mighty Dutchman came to the plate in the ninth, after two of his teammates had succumbed to Boston's play, the dramatic possibilities of the situation forced themselves on the mind of every excited "fan." Great big goose eggs hung from every one of the eight Pittsburgh frames on the score board and it was up to the greatest hitter of the National League to make his mark in the last one. From Boston's frames the three runs stood out in deep relief.
>
> In the gathering gloom, "Big Bill" [Dineen] was shooting the new white ball over so fast that it looked like a will-o'-the-wisp. The big crowd hung on the moment of eager expectation and hardly a sound was heard. Then in a great stage whisper came "Strike Him Out!" as the stands realized no more artistic

conclusion to the great series was possible. "Strike one!" called O'Day and a hysterical yell broke out on the air and then subsided as quickly. "Strike two!" called O'Day, and the whispered "Strike him out" became a wild, incoherent, roaring demand.

Slowly the big pitcher gathered himself up for the effort, slowly he swung his arms above his head. Then the ball shot away like a flash toward the plate where the great Wagner stood, muscles drawn tense waiting for it. The big batsman's mighty shoulders heaved, the stands will swear that his very frame creaked, as he swung his bat with every ounce of power in his body, but the dull thud of the ball, as it nestled in Criger's waiting mitt, told the story.

The game took but one hour, thirty-five minutes, and Boston had prevailed. The *Boston Herald* summed up: "It was the greatest thing for baseball known in years."

GAME 8

Team	1	2	3	4	5	6	7	8	9	R	H	E
Pittsburgh	0	0	0	0	0	0	0	0	0	0	4	3
Boston	0	0	0	2	0	1	0	0	x	3	8	0

As the umpire called the exalted Wagner out, the crowds rushed from the grandstands, jubilant in victory. They raised Dineen, Collins, Stahl, and Parent to their shoulders. (The other Boston players had rushed off the field before the stampede of fans.) The Boston faithful began "to realize the sweet fruits of victory." The Royal Rooters marched around the field in a serpentine fashion before heading off to McGreevey's establishment on Columbus Avenue for a proper celebration of the victory. The *Herald* concluded: "It was a memorable game and one that present fans will recount to their future grandchildren with pride at having been an active participant in it."

After Pittsburgh's Barney Dreyfuss and Fred Clarke congratulated Jimmy Collins and his club, the Pirates' squad headed for the distant gates. "A dozen gray clad figures, alone and unnoticed, walked slowly across the field. Fallen champions . . . they had at last met their Waterloo in Boston. With bat bags on their shoulders . . . they passed beyond the gate." Barney Dreyfuss was magnanimous in his praise for the Boston club. They had won the "World Championship squarely, playing the cleanest kind of baseball." He also congratulated his boys for their efforts—"I am as proud of them as if they had won every game"—and looked forward to a different result in next year's Series: "On behalf of the Pittsburgh club, I wish to thank the press and public of this grand baseball city, for the uniformly kind and fair treatment accorded my players and myself."

The *Pittsburgh Press,* however, was not ready to concede that Boston had the premier club. If only the Pirates had had another pitcher, they would have prevailed. If only the outfield had not been shortened by the overflow crowd, the best team would have won because the Pittsburgh outfielders were "25%" faster than Boston's representatives: "This is admitted by impartial fans who watched the two teams at work." If only . . .

The *Pittsburgh Gazette* blamed the loss on "senseless ground rules [and] bad luck, combined with wet grounds and poor weather." The work of the Pirates on the field was "snappier and cleaner than the victors. . . . They fought nobly and their loss was not one to cause shame."

The *Boston Post* waxed eloquent on the meaning of the Series: "For the game meant more than victory. It was a question of supremacy between two great leagues, a question which for this past two years had agitated the entire baseball world." In fact, despite the hyperbole, outside of Boston and Pittsburgh only the most avid baseball fans took notice of the event. In a few years, however, the World Series would become one of America's great traditions, and the 1903 World Series would be recognized as its genesis.

Although their prospects had appeared bleak after the first few games of the Series, the Boston club had rallied behind steady pitching and timely hitting. Boston gamblers had also rallied and finished the Series in the black. The *Boston Post* reported that Charley Watson cleared $1,500, Charley Lavis $2,000, and Sport Sullivan $8,000. (Other reports suggested that

Sullivan's take had exceeded $20,000.) Despite the heavy gambling, the press insisted that "baseball is the squarest of sports." (Sullivan would later achieve infamy for a much greater sin—arranging the 1919 Black Sox disaster for New York gambler Arnold Rothstein.)

More than one hundred thousand spectators had paid to see the first World Series, an average of more than twelve thousand a game as compared with seventy-five hundred for regular season games. Attention to the Series, at least in the contending towns, "caused people to enthuse who never before took any interest in the game," said the *Pittsburgh Press*. The Series outcome was a great triumph for Ban Johnson, whose entry had bested the champions of the senior circuit. The 1903 World Series cemented in the public's mind that baseball was the national game.

The press commented on how well the rival teams and their respective rooters got on. Only a year earlier at the height of the war between the circuits, no one would have dreamed that American League and National League adherents would share the same field and enjoy the same entertainment.

Gate receipts for the eight games totaled more than $75,000. The receipts were split between the two teams after expenses were deducted. (Each of the two umpires received $50 a game plus their expenses.) The Boston players received 75 percent of their half of the take, each earning $1,182 for the eight-game effort. For many players, this was the equivalent of more than half of their salary for the entire season. Their owner, Henry Killilea, pocketed $6,699.56.

Barney Dreyfuss had promised his players that if they won the Series they would have his owner's share of the winnings as well. To the surprise of many (but not to those who knew of the generosity of the Pirates owner), he threw his share into the player pot of $21,000 even though they had lost. Thus, the losing Pirates players earned more from the Series, $1,316 per player, than the victorious Americans, the only time that would happen in the history of the World Series. Dreyfuss made the World Series checks payable to the players' wives, if they were married, to make sure the money made it home. Dreyfuss also rewarded his stalwart hurler, Deacon Phillippe, with ten shares of stock in the Philadelphia Traction Company, which operated trolley cars in Pittsburgh.

Returning Home

The evening the Boston Americans prevailed in the Series, the British Honourables returned to Boston, completing their tour of North America. Lord Denbigh commented:

> Every place we visited gave a warm welcome. Fall River [Massachusetts] and New York, Montreal, Toronto, Washington and all. But none welcomed us so heartily as Boston had done. We came here first, and so I suppose that Boston considers us as her special guests. I am glad to get back. . . . I think I prefer Boston to any of the cities we've visited.

The *Boston Daily Advertiser* reported that the affection was reciprocal: "The British Honourables took Boston hearts by storm." When their train from Montreal arrived at Boston's North Union Station, a hundred "red-jacketed, gold-laced soldiers swarmed out of the cars." The crowd sang "Auld Lang Syne." After a night in the Hub, the Honourables would sail for London.

On Wednesday, October 14, 1903, most of the Pirates also headed home. They took the 10:40 A.M. train from Trinity Place Station back west. Kitty Bransfield, however, went directly to his home in Worcester, Massachusetts. Captain Fred Clarke planned to take his family to his ranch in Kansas. He looked forward to getting into his farmer's outfit of overalls and high boots and a red bandana around his neck. Tommy Leach planned to move into his new house in Cleveland, said to be quite the "fine home." Catcher Eddie Phelps and his wife planned to spend time in the Adirondack mountains of upstate New York. Word was that Bucky Veil would get married in the off-season. Relief pitcher Gus Thompson headed home to the wilds of Helena, Montana. Ginger Beaumont planned to spend the winter hunting big game near his home in Rochester, Wisconsin, and Deacon Phillippe would do the same in South Dakota.

Barney Dreyfuss planned to spend the winter quietly at home in Pittsburgh with his family. His old friend, Harry Pulliam, the president of the National League, would winter in Florida. Pulliam was said to look tired and worn. The *Pittsburgh Press* reported that "his appearance has caused his friends to worry." They had good reason to be concerned, as he fell deeper into depression. Over the next five years, Pulliam would be subject to unyielding criticism for his decisions from some National League magnates and perpetual malcontents such as John McGraw.

That Wednesday afternoon, the Boston team members took in the Harvard football game against Wesleyan at the new Harvard Stadium, which had a seating capacity of thirty-one thousand, on Soldiers Field. Although Harvard prevailed (17–6), there was gloom on the Cambridge campus because Yale had overpowered Wesleyan 33–0. This did not portend well for the November battle between the Eli and the Crimson. (In fact, their concern was warranted. Yale would shutout Harvard 16–0.)

The Boston players left town before a banquet could be held in their honor that Friday evening at Fanueil Hall. John F. Fitzgerald had chaired a committee to arrange the event, but manager Collins advised him that few members of the club would still be in Boston. The players had served their community well, and for two weeks they had fostered pride and celebration among all segments of the Boston population. They were a gritty bunch of ballplayers who had earned a special place in the pantheon of Boston sports.

Jimmy Collins (who would be signed in November to a new three-year contract to manage the club) left Boston for his home in Buffalo; Freddie Parent left for Sanford, Maine; Candy Lachance went to Waterbury, Connecticut; and Hobe Ferris headed home to Providence, Rhode Island. Buck Freeman returned to western Pennsylvania and Patsy Dougherty to upper New York state. Hero pitcher Bill Dineen returned to Syracuse and Cy Young to his farm in Ohio. Chick Stahl traveled to Chicago, where American League president Ban Johnson announced his pleasure in his American League club for showing that it furnishes "the stronger article of baseball." The Boston club announced that catcher Lou Criger would receive a $500 bonus for his "great work during the past season." Criger returned to Elkhart, Indiana, where he owned a poolroom and betting parlor.

The Sale of the Club

The winter after the victory, owner Henry Killilea decided to sell the Boston American League club. He had enjoyed a profitable year as a magnate, earning more than $50,000, but he had had enough of the Boston media, even then a strongly opinionated press. Killilea was castigated by the papers for having engineered a postseason trade of pitchers with the New York Highlanders (later renamed the Yankees), sending them the twenty-game winner Long Tom Hughes (who had been ineffective in the Series) in exchange for lefty Jesse Tannehill. Killilea had long departed Boston by the time Tannehill hurled a no-hitter for Boston against Chicago on August 17, 1904, one of his twenty-one wins in a splendid season for Boston. Hughes lasted only half a season with the Highlanders, winning seven games against eleven losses before he was traded to Washington.

Any sale of the club would have to be approved by American League president Ban Johnson, who preferred hometown ownership for his circuit's ball clubs. The Boston franchise was the most financially successful in the game, and there were many bidders. A syndicate of Royal Rooters led by Mike Sullivan, a former pitcher for the National League Beaneaters, made an offer that was declined. Former congressman John "Honey Fitz" Fitzgerald offered to purchase the Boston franchise for $150,000, but his bid was vetoed by Ban Johnson. Some have suggested that Johnson was not disposed to having the franchise owned by an Irish politician. It is more likely that Johnson knew Honey Fitz was too independent and beyond his control. Johnson sought a more malleable owner.

On April 19, 1904, the newspapers announced that Henry Killilea had sold the team the prior day to John I. Taylor, the Brahmin son of General Charles Taylor, the publisher and editor-in-chief of the *Boston Globe* since 1873 and the president of the prestigious Algonquin Club. General Taylor knew that his twenty-nine-year-old son needed a diversion from a life otherwise occupied by ladies, parties, tennis, golf, and polo. (John had recently "retired" as advertising manager of the *Globe*.) Taylor purchased the club for his son for $155,000. John I., as he was referred to, was a devoted fanatic of the Boston Americans, which he would rename the Red Sox in 1907 and operate full-time until 1911.

The *Boston Globe*'s front-page story about the sale detailed the course of the negotiations. Ban Johnson, and not Henry Killilea, represented the owner at the table, and the outlines of the deal were set the prior Friday at the Hoffman House in New York City. John I. was "quite agreeable to the chief officer of the American League." Johnson puffed to the newspapers that it had always been his aim to have local ownership of the league's clubs, and Killilea, as a Milwaukee attorney, was the "last of the alien owners." (That does not explain, of course, why Boston native son John F. Fitzgerald was unsuitable.) Killilea was summoned from the Midwest to consummate the deal. Johnson, Taylor, and Killilea dined at the Algonquin Club on the evening of April 18, 1904. The terms of the sale were set.

The next day, Killilea spouted to the press his great pleasure in having been able to "cater to the baseball public" of the Hub and even praised the local newspapers for their loyal support. Taylor assured the press that the club would be run with no changes and "everything will be done to give Boston the best there is in the game." Ban Johnson then left for New York and Henry Killilea for Milwaukee, where he had spent most of his year as the Boston club owner.

The *Boston Globe* would prosper under the leadership of the Taylor family for the entire twentieth century. Although John I. never really took to the family business, other Taylors continued the tradition. Today, although the *Globe* is now a wholly owned subsidiary of The New York Times Company, the Taylor family continues to direct the paper. The current publisher, chairman, and CEO is Benjamin B. Taylor, the great-grandson of General Charles Taylor. In 2002 the *Globe,* through its parent company, participated in the group that purchased the Boston Red Sox.

The 1904 Hiatus

The 1904 season produced an exciting race in the American League that was not decided until the final day's doubleheader between the Boston Americans and the New York Highlanders. John McGraw's New York Giants were the runaway winners of the National League pennant, but McGraw and the Giants' owner, John T. Brush, had announced on July 5 that they had no intention of playing a postseason series with the American League pennant winners: "When we clinch the National League pennant, we'll be champions of the only real major league," said McGraw. Although they would not admit it, it is likely they were afraid the Americans would triumph once again against the National League standard-bearers. John T. Brush was correct when he said: "There is nothing in the constitution or playing rules of the National League which requires its victorious club to submit its championship honors to a contest with a victorious club of a minor league." McGraw's personal hatred of Ban Johnson solidified the Giants' arrogant stand.

Despite this midsummer pronouncement, President John I. Taylor of the victorious Boston Americans wrote to John J. McGraw on October 9, 1904:

> Dear Sir:
>
> As the Boston club to-day won the championship of the American League, I challenge your club to play for the championship of the world. Of course, if you refuse to play, we get the title by default, but I shall prefer to win it on the diamond in a series of five games or more.

McGraw ignored the letter and never responded.

The New York fans were furious with the Giants' decision not to play, but the club's position was long in the making. John Brush was angry about having to share the New York market with an American League entry, especially one such as the Highlanders that played competitive ball. He had had run-ins with Ban Johnson for decades and had strongly opposed the National League's efforts to make peace with the American League in 1903.

McGraw's personal reasons to spurn a postseason championship were well known. He was still peeved by his treatment at the hands of Ban Johnson during his stint as an owner-manager in Baltimore during the American League's inaugural season. McGraw's outrageous antics directed at umpires on the field led to repeated suspensions meted out by Johnson. McGraw was open in his criticism of Johnson: "No man likes to be ordered off the face of the earth like a dog in the presence of his friends. Ballplayers are not a lot of cattle to have the whip cracked over them." Finally, McGraw deviously deserted the new league for the New York Giants and proceeded to undermine the Americans by orchestrating the theft of Baltimore's best players. Johnson berated McGraw publicly for this perfidy. Not one to forget a grudge, McGraw aborted the nascent World Series, announcing that "The Giants will not play a postseason series with the American League champions. Ban Johnson has not been on the level with me personally and the American League management has been crooked more than once." Johnson responded: "No thoughtful patron of baseball can weigh seriously the wild vaporings of this discredited player who was canned out of the American League."

Giants players were incensed at losing the opportunity to earn some additional money. They were a "sore bunch of players," outfielder Mike Donlin told a Cleveland newspaper. Pitcher Joe McGinnity said he was "sore to the core." The New York City press accused Brush of both conceit and cowardice. Brush did not need the extra money a second World Series would have produced—he had cleared $100,000 from the regular season—but his players lost the chance to almost double their annual salaries, already driven down after the end of the economic rivalry between the two leagues.

Rethinking his action during the winter of 1905, Brush drafted a plan for an annual World Series, played as the best-of-seven games. Under the so-called Brush Rules, it was made mandatory for the pennant winners of both leagues to play in the postseason event. The winning club would receive the "emblem of the Professional Base Ball Championship of the World," a pennant, and the players would receive "an appropriate memento, in the form of a button, to be presented to each player of the victorious club." Later, the button prize was elevated to the current diamond-studded ring.

The Brush Rules detailed how World Series receipts would be divided. The new governing body of organized baseball—the National Commission—took 10 percent of the gross. The players on both teams would then be paid from a pool of 40 percent of the balance of the gross receipts of the first four games, thus avoiding any concerns that the players might deliberately extend the Series to earn more money. This pool would be split three-quarters for the players on the winning club, one-quarter for the losers. Management of the competing clubs split the remainder. The site of the first three games would be determined by lot, and the National Commission would determine where the seventh game would be played, if one was necessary. With some minor revisions, the Brush Rules would control baseball's fall pageant for a century. (The only exception was the ill-fated 1994 season, when Acting Commissioner Selig canceled the World Series in the face of a players' strike.)

Barney Dreyfuss

Barney Dreyfuss continued to serve as the owner of the Pirates and a great civic leader in his adopted town of Pittsburgh until his death from pneumonia in 1932. During his more than thirty years as chief executive of the club, Dreyfuss's Pirates won six pennants and two World Series. He designed and constructed Forbes Field in the Oakland district of Pittsburgh at the entrance to bucolic Schenley Park. Forbes Field was located on Forbes Street, named for General John Forbes, the British general who, during the French and Indian Wars, had captured Fort Duquesne from the French and renamed it Fort Pitt.

When Forbes Field opened midseason in 1909—the year the Pirates won the World Series—it was the marvel of baseball. The *Reach Guide* reported in 1910 that "for architectural beauty, imposing size, solid construction and for public comfort and convenience," Forbes Field "has not a superior in the world." The triple-decked park accommodated twenty-five thousand spectators and included telephones and inclined ramps for the convenience of the fans. It became as much an attraction as the ball club, especially for those many years when the Pirates sunk to the bottom half of the National League. Forbes Field would serve as the Pirates' home stadium until 1970.

Nuf Ced McGreevey

Mike McGreevey and his Royal Rooters continued to cheer for their hometown favorites for years to come, singing "Tessie," regaling the local heroes, and ribbing the opposition. For decades, "Tessie" was the standard fare during every Red Sox visit to the World Series. During the 1940s, it was played at Fenway Park on opening day. The Royal Rooters became as much an attraction as the team itself, and saloon keeper Mike McGreevey became a notable public figure.

McGreevey continued his association with the Boston club throughout his life. In 1908, he was hired as a "coach" when the Red Sox went to spring training in Hot Springs, Arkansas. (There is no indication that Nuf Ced Mc-Greevey had any particular baseball skills that he could impart to the Red Sox players, but he was a splendid mascot with a twinkle in his eye.)

McGreevey promoted his Third Base Saloon at 940 Columbus Avenue as "the last stop before you steal home." The left-field wall at the Huntington Avenue Grounds bore his advertisement: "How Can You Get Home Without Reaching 3rd Base? Nuf Ced." The logic seemed unassailable, and McGreevey prospered. His establishment was crammed with baseball memorabilia from ceiling to floor. It relocated to Tremont and Ruggles Streets in 1916 and continued to serve its primarily Irish clientele until Prohibition. McGreevey donated his collection to the Boston Public Library, and his bar became the South End branch of the library in 1923.

The Irish community retained its control over Boston's political establishment throughout the twentieth century. When its sons (and later daughters) graduated from college and professional schools, the Irish became a fixture on Boston's commercial and social scene as well. John L. Sullivan remained an Irish folk legend until his death in 1918. He earned a living by selling his autograph at 10¢ a signature, then lectured widely on the evils of alcohol. Jimmy Collins also maintained a special place in the hearts of the Irish of

Boston. He would play for the Boston Americans until 1907, when he was traded to Philadelphia in exchange for Jack "Schoolboy" Knight, who played only one hundred games for the Boston club.

John I. Taylor, the Red Sox, and Fenway Park

John I. Taylor's reign as owner of the Red Sox had its peaks and valleys. What began as a hobby turned into a full-time job, and Taylor was often at odds with his fellow magnates. In December 1907, he renamed his club the Red Sox, appropriating the moniker abandoned years earlier by Boston's National League club.

He tired of his baseball hobby after the club finished third, fourth, and fifth in 1909, 1910, and 1911. In order to increase the value of the franchise before he sold it, Taylor decided to construct a new ballpark. The Huntington Avenue Grounds stood on land leased from the New York, New Haven and Hartford Railroad, and the Fenway Realty Company, a company he partly owned, held a suitable plot near Landsdowne Street across the Fens about a half-mile to the north. Using his father's money, he broke ground in September 1911 on a new concrete edifice, Fenway Park. Before the stadium was completed, Taylor sold the club, the land, and the unfinished stadium for $150,000. Three seasons later, a nineteen-year-old man-child, left-handed pitcher Babe Ruth, joined the Red Sox. In his six seasons with the club, Ruth would help the team win three World Series, the last in 1918—and the last World Series the Red Sox would win in the twentieth century.

Ban Johnson

Johnson's successful creation of a rival league and its association with the National League in 1903 was the premier business success in baseball history. From 1903 to 1910, attendance at major league games nearly doubled. Interest in the game bubbled throughout society. Perhaps more than anyone else, Ban Johnson should be credited with creating the modern professional sports enterprise.

Although he was the undisputed czar of baseball for almost two decades, Johnson never served as the actual chairman of the ruling National Commission. All knew, however, that his word was the law. He had repeated run-ins with owners and players, but he regularly prevailed. He led the magnates in their successful battle against Federal League owners who in 1914 challenged the established circuits, as Johnson had done successfully at the start of the century.

Johnson could not withstand the public pressure surrounding the conspiracy of the 1919 White Sox and the constant bickering among owners that ensued. The magnates finally begged the autocratic federal judge Kenesaw Mountain Landis to take sole possession of executive power of baseball. Johnson remained the nominal head of the American League, but he had lost control to a man who would lord over baseball for the next twenty-five years.

Johnson's counterpart in the National League, Harry Pulliam, was not as fortunate. Throughout his tenure as league president from 1902 until 1908, he was ensnarled in disputes. Pulliam was despondent after addressing a nasty name-calling incident between John J. McGraw and Barney Dreyfuss. In May 1905, after McGraw was thrown out of a Giants game against the visiting Pirates (not an unusual occurrence for the Little Napoleon), McGraw goaded the Pirates' owner. The incident became known as the "Hey Barney!" affair. McGraw heckled Dreyfuss about welching on bets and controlling the umpires, and Dreyfuss responded in kind. A few days later, Dreyfuss filed a formal complaint against McGraw with Pulliam. McGraw denied the entire incident (although it was heard by the whole crowd at the Polo Grounds). Pulliam fined McGraw, and the press had a field day taking sides in the contretemps. Finally, a hometown New York court set aside McGraw's fine as "un-American."

Further disputes with owners and players in 1908 finally felled Pulliam. He took a leave of absence from his position in February 1909 and was replaced by John A. Heydler, the secretary-treasurer of the National League. During his leave, Pulliam traveled across the country and seemed to have overcome his despondency. He resumed work as the league president. On July 28, 1909, he came into work at 9:30 A.M. and started going through a pile of correspondence. At 1:00 P.M. he left the office, telling his secretary he did not feel well. He went directly to his room at the New York Athletic Club, put a pistol to his head, and committed suicide.

Reverend Billy Sunday's Tabernacle

Fenway Park replaced the Huntington Avenue Grounds as the home of the Red Sox in 1912, and the wooden ballpark was demolished. The lot returned to its earlier use as a site for traveling circuses and shows. The Ringling Brothers and Barnum and Bailey circus pitched its tents annually on the large open field. Reverend Billy Sunday built a huge terra-cotta brick and steel structure on the field for his evangelical crusades of 1916 and 1917. More than 1.5 million people attended Sunday's riveting sermons, almost sixty-five thousand of whom came forward to declare themselves converted.

Rudolph Morris, in his informal history of Northeastern University, offered the following description of Sunday's tabernacle:

> It was an enormous structure. . . . The floor was dirt with a thick covering of sawdust, and the seats were long, backless benches. We sat in the middle of the hall with the outer walls so far away I could vaguely see a large group of people sitting back of the pulpit. I asked Miss Foss who they were, and she answered with some asperity: "They are Baptists. They always get the best seats."

Billy Sunday first rose to public prominence as a baseball player during the 1880s. His smooth play in the outfield over eight seasons with the Chicago and Pittsburgh franchises of the National League had made him a crowd favorite, although his lifetime batting average of .248 suggests he was a better evangelist than ballplayer. He prepared for his life's work by teaching Sunday school during the off-season. He was always a great supporter of the national pastime, opining from the pulpit: "All this talk of baseball being crooked is an unmitigated lie." When such an edict came from one of the nation's exceptional evangelists, it had considerable persuasive power.

During the 1950s, Northeastern University acquired the land where Sunday's tabernacle and the Huntington Avenue Grounds had stood and constructed a campus that now serves more than twenty thousand students. At the core of the campus, near the spot where the pitcher's mound once stood, stands a life-sized statute of the great Cy Young, hunched over and looking for the catcher's sign. On Huntington Avenue where the grounds' left-field wall stood, the university constructed Cabot Physical Education Center. In December 2000, in recognition of a lifetime of dedicated service, the university named the facility where Northeastern's basketball and volley-ball teams play the Bernard and Jolane Solomon Court, on the spot where Bunny Solomon's father Sam had sneaked into the 1903 World Series almost a century earlier.

Conclusion

The story of the 1903 World Series represents a microcosm of American life at the turn of the twentieth century. It is the story of some superb athletes: Cy Young, Honus Wagner, Jimmy Collins, Fred Clarke, Bill Dineen, and Dea-con Phillippe. It is the story of the American immigrants: the Yankees and Brahmins, the Irish and the Jews. It is the story of Boston and of Pittsburgh. It is, of course, the story of America.

The 1903 World Series is important because it was the first. Every Series offers exciting games to interested spectators and viewers tuned in around the world. But there is something special about being the first occurrence of an event that continues on for more than a century, especially in a country where the history for European settlement goes back only a few hundred years and culture spins around each decade. By the start of the twentieth century, America had moved from a predominantly rural agrarian society to one based on urban manufacturing. Its cities were teeming with im-migrants—a polyglot from around the world. Baseball was one of the few things these urban dwellers shared.

Boston is a special American city, steeped in historical significance as well as baseball fanaticism. But other American cities offered similar attractions.

Boston happened to be where the first World Series began and ended. That is reason enough to focus on the people who filled its various neighborhoods and enjoyed the national game. It was a very different place from Pittsburgh, as we have seen—not better, only different.

Baseball's fanatics were at their best during the 1903 World Series. They were more than mere spectators to an event. They participated in the games through their singing and cheering, and they were remarkably well behaved. They led very separate lives outside of the ballpark. Inside the wooden walls, however, they joined in common purpose—to cheer their heroes on to victory.

Notes

The Boston and Pittsburgh newspapers provided the primary source of data on the 1903 World Series and the rhythms of life at the turn of the twentieth century. The *Boston Herald* proved particularly helpful in its description of spectators at the baseball contests, and the *Boston Globe* offered superb coverage of the visit of the British Honourable Artillery Company. Other references in the text are taken from the *Boston Post*. The Boston dailies seemed more partisan than their Pittsburgh counterparts, at least until the Americans bested the Pirates and the Smoky City media cried "foul." I used the *Pittsburgh Gazette* and the *Pittsburgh Press* as the main research sources for material about that city.

I have explored the history of America's game in two earlier books, *Legal Bases: Baseball and the Law* and *The Money Pitch: Baseball Free Agency and Salary Arbitration,* both published by Temple University Press. The classic texts on baseball history remain two works by Harold Seymour—*Baseball: The Golden Age* and *Baseball: The Early Years.* They are the only truly comprehensive works on America's game. The recent compendium by Glenn Stout and Richard Johnson, *Red Sox Century: One Hundred Years of Red Sox Baseball* (2000), is the definitive work on the Boston club's history. Biographies of Honus Wagner by Dennis and Jeanne DeValeria and of Cy Young by Reed Browning filled in the gaps in the standard histories.

Many primary and secondary texts provided insight into the lives of the Brahmins, Irish, and Jews. Most useful were *The Education of Henry Adams* by the Brahmin chieftain himself; Doris Kearns Goodwin's *The Fitzgeralds and the Kennedys;* and Oscar Handlin's monumental *Boston's Immigrants: 1790–1880.* Samuel Solomon's son, Bunny Solomon, shared with me the stories of his family's immigration to America and his father's lifelong devotion to baseball. Bunny Solomon is an Emeritus Trustee of Northeastern University, a loyal alumnus, and a lifelong Boston Braves fan.

Bibliography

Books

Abrams, Roger I. *Legal Bases: Baseball and the Law*. Philadelphia: Temple University Press, 1998.

———. *The Money Pitch: Baseball Free Agency and Salary Arbitration*. Philadelphia: Temple University Press, 2000.

Adams, Henry. *The Education of Henry Adams*. 1907; rept., Boston: Houghton Mifflin, 2000.

Adelman, Melvin L. *A Sporting Time: New York City and the Rise of Modern Athletics, 1820–1870*. Urbana: University of Illinois Press, 1986.

Alexander, Charles C. *John McGraw*. Lincoln: University of Nebraska Press, 1988.

———. *Rogers Hornsby: A Biography*. New York: Henry Holt and Company, 1995.

Allen, Frederick Lewis. *The Big Change: America Transforms Itself, 1900–1950*. New Brunswick, N.J.: Transaction Publishers, 1993.

Amory, Cleveland. *The Proper Bostonians*. Orleans, Mass.: Parnassus Imprints, 1947.

Ben-Sasson, H. H. *A History of the Jewish People*. Cambridge: Harvard University Press, 1976.

Bernheim, Isaac Wolfe, *The Story of the Bernheim Family*. Louisville, Ky.: John P. Morton & Company, 1910.

Birmingham, Stephen. *Real Lace: America's Irish Rich*. New York: Harper & Row, 1973.

Blewett, Mary H. *Men, Women and Work: Class, Gender and Protest in the New England Shoe Industry, 1780–1910*. Urbana: University of Illinois Press, 1988.

Bodner, John, Roger Simon, and Michael P. Weber. *Lives of Their Own: Blacks, Italians and Poles in Pittsburgh, 1900–1960*. Urbana: University of Illinois Press, 1983.

Browning, Reed. *Cy Young: A Baseball Life*. Amherst: University of Massachusetts Press, 2000.

Couvares, Francis G. *The Remaking of Pittsburgh: Class and Culture in an Industrialized City, 1877–1919*. Albany: State University of New York Press, 1984.

Crichton, Judy. *America 1900*. New York: Henry Holt, 1998.

Cromwell, Adelaide M. *The Other Brahmins: Boston's Black Upper Class, 1750–1950*. Fayetteville: University of Arkansas Press, 1994.

Deford, Frank. *Casey on the Loose*. New York: Viking Penguin, 1989.

DeValeria, Dennis, and Jeanne Burke DeValeria. *Honus Wagner: A Biography*. Pittsburgh: University of Pittsburgh Press, 1998.

Devaney, John, and Burt Goldblatt. *The World Series: A Complete Pictorial History.* New York: Rand McNally, 1972.

Dubois, W. E. B. *Autobiography of W. E. B. DuBois: A Soliloquy on Viewing My Life from the Last Decade of Its First Century.* New York: International Publishers, 1968.

———. *The Souls of Black Folks: Essays and Sketches.* Chicago: A. C. McClurg & Co., 1903.

Duis, Perry R. *The Saloon: Public Drinking in Chicago and Boston, 1880–1920.* Urbana: University of Illinois Press, 1983.

Feldman, Jacob S. *The Jewish Experience in Western Pennsylvania: A History, 1775–1945.* Pittsburgh: Historical Society of Western Pennsylvania, 1986.

Ginsburg, Daniel E. *The Fix Is In: A History of Baseball Gambling and Game Fixing Scandals.* Jefferson, N.C.: McFarland & Company, 1995.

Goodwin, Doris Kearns. *The Fitzgeralds and the Kennedys: An American Saga.* New York: St. Martin's Press, 1987.

Gorn, Elliott, and Warren Goldstein. *A Brief History of American Sports.* New York: Hill and Wang, 1993.

Handlin, Oscar. *Boston's Immigrants: 1790–1880.* Cambridge: Belknap Press of Harvard University Press, 1991.

Hardy, Stephen. *How Boston Played: Sport, Recreation, and Community, 1865–1915.* Boston: Northeastern University Press, 1982.

Hittner, Arthur D. *Honus Wagner: The Life of Baseball's "Flying Dutchman."* Jefferson, N.C.: McFarland & Company, 1996.

Howe, Mark A. DeWolfe. *Boston: The Place and the People.* New York: Macmillan Company, 1912.

Johnson, Richard A. *A Century of Boston Sports.* Boston: Northeastern University Press, 2000.

Katzman, David M., and William M. Tuttle, Jr. *Plain Folk: The Life Stories of Undistinguished Americans.* Urbana: University of Illinois Press, 1982.

Kirsch, George B. *The Creation of American Team Sports: Baseball and Cricket, 1838–72.* Urbana: University of Illinois Press, 1989.

Koppett, Leonard. *Koppett's Concise History of Major League Baseball.* Philadelphia: Temple University Press, 1998.

Laxton, Edward. *The Famine Ships: The Irish Exodus to America.* New York: Henry Holt, 1998.

Lieb, Frederick G. *The Baseball Story.* New York: G. P. Putnam's Sons, 1950.

———. *The Story of the World Series.* New York: G. P. Putnam's Sons, 1965.

Lorant, Stephan. *Pittsburgh: The Story of an American City.* Pittsburgh: Esselmont Books, 1999.

Lovett, James D'Wolf. *Old Boston Boys and the Games They Played.* Cambridge, Mass.: Riverside Press, 1906.

Mitchel, John. *The Last Conquest of Ireland (Perhaps).* Glasgow: Cameron, Ferguson & Company, 1861.

Morison, Samuel Eliot. *One Boy's Boston, 1887–1903.* Boston: Houghton Mifflin, 1962.

Murdock, Eugene C. *Ban Johnson: Czar of Baseball.* Westport, Conn.: Greenwood Press, 1982.

Nemec, David. *The Official Rules of Baseball: An Anecdotal Look at the Rules of Baseball and How They Came To Be*. New York: Lyons Press, 1994.

Rader, Benjamin G. *Baseball: A History of America's Game*. Urbana: University of Illinois Press, 1992.

Riess, Steven A. *City Games: The Evolution of American Urban Society and the Rise of Sports*. Urbana: University of Illinois Press, 1989.

———. *Touching Base: Professional Baseball and American Culture in the Progressive Era*. Urbana: University of Illinois Press, 1999.

Ritter, Lawrence S. *The Glory of Their Times: The Story of the Early Days of Baseball Told by the Men Who Played It*. New York: Vintage Books, 1985.

Seymour, Harold. *Baseball: The Early Years*. New York: Oxford University Press, 1990.

———. *Baseball: The Golden Age*. New York: Oxford University Press, 1971.

———. *Baseball: The People's Game*. New York: Oxford University Press, 1990.

Skolnik, Richard C. *Baseball and the Pursuit of Innocence: A Fresh Look at the Old Ball Game*. College Station: Texas A & M Press, 1994.

Smith, Robert. *World Series: The Games and the Players*. Garden City, N.Y.: Doubleday, 1967.

Soos, Troy. *Before the Curse: The Glory Days of New England Baseball, 1858–1918*. Hyannis, Mass.: Parnassus Imprints, 1997.

Spalding, Albert. *Guide to Baseball*. Published annually in Chicago by Albert Spalding.

Stout, Glenn, and Richard A. Johnson. *Red Sox Century: One Hundred Years of Red Sox Baseball*. Boston: Houghton Mifflin, 2000.

Sullivan, Dean A. *Early Innings: A Documentary History of Baseball, 1825–1908*. Lincoln: University of Nebraska Press, 1995.

Traxel, David. *1898: The Birth of the American Century*. New York: Vintage Books, 1998.

Tunis, John Roberts. *A Measure of Independence*. New York: Atheneum, 1964.

Veblen, Thorstein. *The Theory of the Leisure Class: An Economic Study of Institutions*. 1899; rept., New York: Penguin Classics, 1959.

Voight, David Quentin. *American Baseball: From the Gentleman's Sport to the Commissioner System*. University Park: Pennsylvania State University Press, 1983.

Wallace, Alfred Russel. *The Wonderful Century: Its Successes and Failures*. London: Sonnenschein, 1898.

Ward, Geoffrey C., and Ken Burns. *Baseball: An Illustrated History*. New York: Alfred A. Knopf, 1994.

Weiler, Paul C. *Leveling the Playing Field*. Cambridge: Harvard University Press, 2000.

White, G. Edward. *Creating the National Pastime: Baseball Transforms Itself, 1903–1953*. Princeton, N.J.: Princeton University Press, 1996.

Woods, Robert A., ed. *Americans in Process: A Settlement Study*. Boston: Houghton, Mifflin and Company, 1903.

Periodicals

Appleton's Journal, April 1869–December 1881.
Atlantic Monthly, November 1857–December 1901.
Boston Globe, September 1–November 1, 1903.
Boston Herald, September 1–November 1, 1903.
Boston Post, September 1–November 1, 1903.
Century Magazine, November 1881–October 1899.
Harper's Weekly, June 1850–April 1899.
Ladies' Repository, January 1841–December 1876.
Pittsburgh Gazette, September 1–November 1, 1903.
Pittsburgh Press, September 1–November 1, 1903.

Index

Photograph Credits

The photographs in this book are reproduced courtesy of the following.

The statue of Cy Young: Northeastern University
The Huntington Avenue Grounds: Boston Public Library
Ban Johnson: Boston Public Library
John I. Taylor: Boston Public Library
John Fitzgerald and the Royal Rooters: Boston Public Library
Exposition Park: Carnegie Library of Pittsburgh
Honus Wagner: Carnegie Library of Pittsburgh
The Solomon family: Bernard Solomon
The Americans and the Pirates: Boston Public Library